The
Promise of
Representative
Bureaucracy

Bureaucracies, Public Administration, and Public Policy

Kenneth J. Meier
Series Editor

The Promise of Representative Bureaucracy

Diversity and Responsiveness in a Government Agency

Sally Coleman Selden

M.E. Sharpe
Armonk, New York
London, England

Library of Congress Cataloging-in-Publication Data

Selden, Sally Coleman, 1966–
The promise of representative bureaucracy: diversity and
responsiveness in a government agency / by Sally Coleman Selden.
        p.   cm.—(Bureaucracies, public administration, and
                        public policy)
        Includes bibliographical references and index.
ISBN 0-7656-0055-2 (cloth : alk. paper)—ISBN 0-7656-0056-0 (pbk. : alk. paper)
        1. United States. Farmers Home Administration.   2. Bureaucracy.
                3. Democracy.   I. Title.   II. Series.
                        HG2051.U5C558   1997
                353.5′52736′0973—dc21   97-12695
                                CIP
        Printed in the United States of America

The paper used in this publication meets the minimum requirements of
American National Standard for Information Sciences—
Permanence of Paper for Printed Library Materials,
ANSI Z 39.48-1984.

BM (c)   10   9   8   7   6   5   4   3   2   1
BM (p)   10   9   8   7   6   5   4   3   2   1

To my family

Contents

List of Tables and Figures

Tables

Figures

Foreword

The M.E. Sharpe series in Bureaucracy, Public Policy, and Public Administration is designed as a forum for the best work on bureaucracy and its role in public policy and governance. Although the series is open with regard to approach, methods, and perspectives, especially sought are three types of research. First, the series hopes to attract empirical studies of bureaucracy. Public administration has long been viewed as a theoretical and methodological backwater of political science. This view persists despite a recent flurry of research. The series seeks to place public administration at the forefront of empirical analysis within political science. Second, the series is interested in conceptual work that attempts to clarify theoretical issues, set an agenda for research, or provide a focus for professional debates. Third, the series seeks manuscripts that challenge the conventional wisdom about how bureaucracies influence public policy or the role of public administration in governance.

I am very pleased to include in the M.E. Sharpe series Sally Coleman Selden's *The Promise of Representative Bureaucracy*. A past winner of the Leonard White award for the best dissertation in public administration, *The Promise of Representative Bureaucracy* shows how first-class research in public administration should be done. It is a rigorous empirical study that breaks new ground theoretically. At the same time it has practical implications for the day-to-day operation of bureaucracies. *The Promise of Representative Bureaucracy* should be read by every graduate student in public administration as a blueprint for the process of research in public administration.

Many scholars have proposed that representative bureaucracy is a way to reconcile the need for bureaucracy with the demands of a democratic state. Representative bureaucracy is a theory that suggests bureaucratic values are a function of the social origins of the bureaucrats. If, the theory suggests, bureaucracies can be made broadly representative of the people, then the values held by bureaucrats will correspond with those of the general public. Political controls are less necessary in such a situation because as bureaucrats maximize their own values, they produce policies that will benefit the broader public.

Professor Selden's contribution is to link representative bureaucracy back to the broader demands of the organization. Many contend that representative bureaucracy will rarely work because organizations socialize their employees to advocate the interests of the organization. Professor Selden examines the roles that bureaucrats play within an organization. Some bureaucrats, she finds, accept the role of representing minority interests in the organization and resist the other socialization pressures in the organization. While many such bureaucrats are minorities, many are not. A person's perceived role in the organization, as a result, becomes a more powerful predictor of behavior than race or minority status.

In her study of the Federal Home Administration, Professor Selden finds that, because they have more individuals who accept the role of minority representative, regional offices with more minority employees are more likely to grant loans to minority clientele. Hers joins a small number of other studies to find that bureaucratic representation makes a significant difference in the lives of citizens. This finding moves debates concerning affirmative action beyond the question of access to jobs or patronage to broader questions of the responsiveness of bureaucracy to the entire population.

The Promise of Representative Bureaucracy is relevant to many subfields in public administration. Organizational behavior scholars will find the discussion of role and advocacy related to their work. Students of personnel administration will find much to inform their knowledge of recruitment, motivation, and employee performance. Individuals concerned with policy implementation will see one of the first studies to incorporate bureaucratic commitment in an empirical study. And students of democracy and bureaucracy will find this work central to their concerns about responsive administration. The primary contribution of *The Promise of Representative Bureaucracy*, however, is that it is a sterling example of how research in public administration ought to be done.

Kenneth J. Meier
University of Wisconsin–Madison

Preface

The concept of representative bureaucracy suggests that a bureaucracy that employs a cross section of American society will produce policy outcomes and outputs that reflect the interests and needs of all groups. The primary question addressed in this study is whether passive representation, or the extent to which a bureaucracy employs people of diverse demographic backgrounds, leads to active representation, or the pursuit of policies reflecting the interests and desires of those people.

The linkage between passive representation and policy outputs in the Farmers Home Administration's (FmHA) Rural Housing Loans program is the basis for this analysis. Analysis of FmHA districts reveals that the passive representation of African Americans, Hispanics, and Asians significantly affected the allocation of loan eligibility decisions favoring those groups.

In order to better understand the process by which active representation follows from passive representation, the second part of the study shifted the unit of analysis from FmHA districts to FmHA county supervisors. An integrative model was developed based on the three primary components of representative bureaucracy: passive representation; attitudes/role perceptions (potential for active representation); and active representation. The model also incorporated other factors suggested in the literature to affect these relationships. FmHA county supervisors in southern states were surveyed about their personal backgrounds, professional and community involvement, and attitudes toward their job responsibilities.

The results yielded considerable support for the major theoretical linkages suggested in the representative bureaucracy literature. First, demographic characteristics and other socialization experiences significantly shaped an individual's attitude toward assuming a minority advocacy or representative role. Socialization to the agency did not overwhelm the importance of one's demographic background in structuring attitudes. Second, the extent to which a county supervisor perceived his or her role as an advocate of minority interests significantly influenced the percentage of eligibility decisions favoring minorities and the extent to which the supervisor publicized the loans program in the minority community.

Acknowledgments

I am especially grateful to a number of persons who have provided support and advice in writing this book. Several people have read all or part of this manuscript in one draft or another, and I owe a special debt to them for their comments and suggestions: Ed Kellough, Jeff Brudney, Hal Rainey, Larry O'Toole, Jerry Legge, Chilik Yu, Susan Zlomke, Ralph Hummel, Carolyn Ban, and Ken Meier. I wish to extend a special thank you to Ed Kellough, who directed the dissertation from which this book grew. As a teacher, adviser, and friend, he provided invaluable advice and feedback as I developed this manuscript. I am also deeply indebted to Jeff Brudney, who was always willing to take time from his own work to help me. Many of the ideas expressed in this book were shaped greatly through conversations with Chilik Yu and the research and ideas of Ken Meier. The University of Georgia's Carl Vinson Institute of Government provided me with substantial support in this research endeavor. In particular, I would like to express my gratitude to Rick Campbell, Dan Durning, Becky Hill, Joni Bertsch, and Melanie Hardman. The research assistance of Doug Ballard, Tara Webster, and Mike Korb was invaluable. I will be forever appreciative to the Farmers Home Administration employees who took time from their hectic schedules to provide data and documents, endure numerous questions over the phone, and complete a rather lengthy survey. This book would not have been possible without their cooperation. Finally, I would like to thank Frank Selden. His support, encouragement, and understanding have enabled me to complete this project.

List of Abbreviations

ADA	Americans for Democratic Action
AFDC	Aid to Families with Dependent Children
AMA	American Medical Association
CRC	Commission on Civil Rights
DOA	Department of Agriculture
DOD	Department of Defense
EEOC	Equal Employment Opportunity Commission
EMR	educable mentally retarded
ERA	Equal Rights Amendment
FBI	Federal Bureau of Investigation
FEMA	Federal Emergency Management Agency
FmHA	Farmers Home Administration
FTC	Federal Trade Commission
GAO	General Accounting Office
GS	General Schedule
GSA	General Services Administration
HMDA	Home Mortgage Disclosure Act
HUD	Department of Housing and Urban Development
NASA	National Aeronautics and Space Administration
NIH	National Institutes of Health

OMB   Office of Management and Budget
OPM   Office of Personnel Management
OSHA   Occupational Safety and Health Administration

SBA   Small Business Administration
SES   Senior Executive Service
SMSA   Standard Metropolitan Statistical Area

TMR   trainable mentally retarded

USDA   U.S. Department of Agriculture

VA   Department of Veteran Affairs

The
Promise of
Representative
Bureaucracy

1

Bureaucracy As a Representative Institution

Decision making that values diversity multiplies the points of access to government, disperses power, and struggles to ensure a full and developed rational dialogue. Public policy then becomes "the equilibrium reached in the group struggle at any given moment."

—Lani Guinier (1994, 175)

Administrative decisions are often, in a broad sense, political decisions. In government departments and agencies, for example, administrators charged with responsibility for program implementation ultimately shape the nature of many public policies.[1] For example, Charles T. Goodsell (1985, 41) found substantial variation in the "tone of voice" used in Aid to Families with Dependent Children (AFDC) food stamp application forms and instructions. Some offices addressed potential clients positively in their program literature, while others were negative and threatening. The tone of the materials sends a powerful message to potential applicants about the organization's climate and attitude toward clients. Government bureaucrats exert influence over the formation of public policy every day, often in small ways, but just as frequently in larger ways (Krislov 1974). Consequently, the control of administrative power in public service is extremely important, especially in a democratic system. Traditionally, scholars have focused on formal constitutional mechanisms and less formal strategies emphasizing public access, efficiency, and competence to reconcile administrative power and democracy. Today, however, the problem of ensuring administrative responsibility and responsiveness to the public remains a major concern in public administration (Gilbert 1959; Larson 1973; Meier 1993b; Mosher 1982; Waldo 1952).

Problems of bureaucratic responsibility emerge because classified civil servants are at least three steps removed from the American electorate (Mosher 1982). Elected officials appoint top-level administrators who in turn direct organizations staffed by civil service employees. Furthermore, the civil service personnel system is designed to protect employees from political pressure. Employees in the classified service cannot be disciplined, transferred, or promoted for political reasons. As a result, some scholars contend that presidential and congressional oversight alone are inadequate means of ensuring bureaucratic responsibility (Gilbert 1959). When this concern is coupled with the fact that civil servants exercise considerable administrative discretion at all levels of the public bureaucracy, problems of accountability and responsibility become critical.

As a consequence, a number of scholars have endorsed the view that bureaucratic power to mold public policy can be made more responsive to public interests (and will therefore better serve democratic principles) if the personnel in the bureaucracy reflect the public served, in characteristics such as race, ethnicity, and gender (Rourke 1978, 396). This idea forms the rationale for the theory of "representative bureaucracy." The argument is premised on the belief that such attributes lead to certain early socialization experiences that in turn give rise to attitudes and values that ultimately help to shape the behavior and decisions of individual bureaucrats (Kranz 1976; Krislov 1974; Saltzstein 1979). Proponents contend that representative bureaucracy provides a means of fostering equity in the policy process by helping to ensure that all interests are represented in the formulation and implementation of policies and programs (Denhardt and deLeon 1995; Saltzstein 1979). According to Samuel Krislov (1974, 21), a prominent scholar on the subject, "the greater the degree of discretion imputed to a bureaucracy, the more vigorous its functions, the stronger the need for the type of accountability and sense of responsibility implied by the call for representativeness."

The Issue of Bureaucratic Representation

J. Donald Kingsley's (1944) book, *Representative Bureaucracy*, is the first work to systematically examine the issue of public work force

representation. Kingsley, who studied the operation of the public service in Great Britain, advanced the notion that the civil service should
reflect the characteristics of the ruling social class because the civil
service must be sympathetic to the concerns of the dominant political
leadership. Kingsley's work was grounded on the notion that the representativeness of the public bureaucracy should be measured in terms of
social class. Operating from that premise, V. Subramanian (1967) documented middle-class dominance in the bureaucracies of several na-
tions, including Great Britain, France, India, and the United States.
Later work by Kenneth J. Meier (1975) focusing on the American civil
service measured bureaucratic representativeness in terms of a variety
of factors such as age, education, income, size of birthplace, social
class, region of birth, and father's occupation. Subsequent interest in
the racial, ethnic, and gender-based representativeness of the American
bureaucracy emerged in part because of the relative underrepresentation of minorities and women in middle and higher levels of the civil
service and because important attitudinal and opinion chasms often
form along racial, ethnic, and gender lines.

The central tenet of the concept of representative bureaucracy is that
passive representation, or the extent to which a bureaucracy employs
people of diverse demographic backgrounds, leads to active representation, or the pursuit of policies reflecting the interests and desires of
those people (Meier 1993b; Meier and Stewart 1992; Mosher 1982).
For example, African-American administrators may be more supportive of Equal Employment Opportunity Commission (EEOC) policies
than their white counterparts, or Hispanic police officers may be more
empathetic toward Hispanic suspects than non-Hispanic officers. This
is plausible because of the belief that individuals of like backgrounds
undergo similar socialization experiences. Those experiences lead to
the formation of attitudes and values that are subsequently linked to
behavior. The theory suggests that minority administrators, for example, will share attitudes and values with minorities in the general population and will therefore act to represent minority interests when
opportunities to do so arise in the policy process.

Some scholars have argued, however, that the link between demographic background and attitudes/values is weakened or overcome by
organizational socialization (Meier and Nigro 1976; Mosher 1982).
Socialization is an ongoing learning process that continues once an
individual enters an organizational setting and may be used to create a

culture or environment that encourages organizational commitment and loyalty. When the organization's mission or culture does not emphasize minority or female interests, socialization to the organization may weaken the link between the demographic background of administrators and active representation of minorities and women (Meier and Nigro 1976; Romzek and Hendricks 1982). For example, representation of women and minorities is not central to the mission of the National Institutes of Health or the Central Intelligence Agency. In such agencies, the acceptance of organizational norms and values will likely decrease representative bureaucracy. Agencies with a mission that includes representation of particular groups, such as the EEOC and the Commission on Civil Rights (CRC), are more likely to inculcate in employees values that include active representation of particular groups.

Benefits of Representative Bureaucracy

A bureaucracy that reflects the diversity of the general population implies a symbolic commitment to equal access to power (Gallas 1985; Meier 1993c; Mosher 1982; Wise 1990). The symbolic role results from both the personal characteristics of distinctive group members, and the assumption that because of these characteristics, the bureaucracy has had experiences in common with other members of that group (Guinier 1994). When members of distinctive groups become public officials, they become legitimate actors in the political process with the ability to shape public policy.

Groups previously not represented may provide genuine expertise, valid information, and more accurate reflections of group preferences (Kranz 1976). To a degree, individuals are limited in their understanding of an issue by their own experiences and frames of reference. When a group is not represented, its concerns and preferences are less likely to be voiced and brought to bear on decisions rendered. A more diverse decision-making entity suggests that a wider range of perspectives will be considered. The presence of underrepresented groups should enhance the majority group's empathic understanding and responsiveness to previously underrepresented or excluded groups (Kranz 1976).

A representative bureaucracy should also influence how items are prioritized on the agenda (Kingdon 1984; Guy 1992). According to

John Kingdon (1984, 160), agendas change either because "incumbents in positions of authority change their priorities and push new agenda items; or the personnel in those positions changes, bringing new priorities onto the agenda by virtue of the turnover." As the share of women and minorities in decision-making positions increases, subjects of particular interest to these groups have a greater chance of becoming a priority on the agenda (Guy 1992). Some scholars, for example, have gauged increased responsiveness by examining the discourse on and adoption of policies and practices that target specific groups (Tamerius 1995). A bureaucracy that reflects the demographic composition of society will incorporate a greater spectrum of opinions and preferences into the agenda-setting and decision-making processes and, as a result, should be more responsive to those groups (Kranz 1976).

Several scholars also suggest that groups previously underrepresented or unrepresented will be more closely bound to the agency as their representation increases and, as a result, they will be more inclined to cooperate and to co-produce with bureaucratic agencies (Kranz 1976; Shafritz, Hyde, and Rosenbloom 1986). Potential clients, for example, may be more apt to participate in government programs when they identify and are comfortable with program administrators (Hadwiger 1973). Similarly, they may avoid taking part in programs if they are intimated by or feel awkward around program personnel.

The last benefit to be highlighted is that a more representative bureaucracy will lead to a more efficient use of human resources (Kranz 1976). Previously excluded groups, such as minority females, are readily available in the labor pool.

Since at least the 1960s, government jurisdictions in the United States have pursued a number of equal employment opportunity and affirmative action strategies designed to promote work force diversity. Recently, these efforts have been under siege, and questions have been raised about the fairness of affirmative action policies designed to advance the opportunities of previously underrepresented groups. To inform policy makers' decisions regarding the benefits of a diversified work force, however, it is important to consider some of the empirical questions that emerge from the concept of representative bureaucracy.

The first issue that arises is whether or not the bureaucracy broadly reflects the demographic characteristics of the population, and what factors explain variations in representation. Are people of diverse racial and ethnic backgrounds employed? Are women as well as men employed in important positions? Following these questions is the issue of whether or not increasing work force diversity makes a difference in organizational operations and policies. Has increasing female, minority, and ethnic employment had an impact on policy outputs?

Empirical Research on Representative Bureaucracy

There are three major components to the theory of representative bureaucracy:

> Passive Representation
> → Potential for Active Representation (Values & Attitudes)
> → Active Representation

Empirical research on the topic follows these components closely. Some researchers have focused on the demographic composition of the bureaucracy as a test of representation, some have explored attitude congruence between bureaucrats and represented groups, and others have examined the effect of minority representation on policy outputs and outcomes. The bulk of previous empirical research has concentrated on passive representation, that is, whether or not the bureaucracy broadly reflects the composition of society in terms of gender, race, and ethnicity (Hellriegel and Short 1972; Nachmias and Rosenbloom 1973; Gibson and Yeager 1975; Grabosky and Rosenbloom 1975; Meier 1975; Hall and Saltzstein 1977; Rose and Chia 1978; Cayer and Sigelman 1980; Smith 1980; Dometrius 1984; Lewis 1988; Kellough 1990a; Kim 1993; Page 1994). Also, a number of scholars have looked at determinants of female, minority, and ethnic employment levels in municipalities and the federal government (Dye and Renick 1981; Eisinger 1982; Welch et al. 1983; Riccucci 1986; Saltzstein 1986; Stein 1986; Mladenka 1989a, 1989b, 1991; Kellough 1990a; Kellough and Elliott 1992; Kim 1993; Cornwell and Kellough 1994).

A second category of research has explored the relationship between demographic characteristics and bureaucrats' attitudes. These studies have yielded contradictory results, which may be due in part to different approaches used to measure attitude congruence. For example, in ten of the twelve policy areas examined, Kenneth Meier and Lloyd Nigro (1976) found that organizational socialization was more important than demographic factors in explaining attitudes. In one case, welfare, the influences of social origins and organizational socialization were the same. On the issue of improving the conditions of minorities, demographic factors (including race) were more important than organizational socialization. David Rosenbloom and Jeannette Featherstonhaugh (1977), on the other hand, concluded that despite the effects of agency socialization, social characteristics continued to influence the attitudes of civil servants. They found that African-American civil servants tended to hold attitudes similar to African Americans in the general population when compared to white federal bureaucrats.

Empirical research examining the impact of passive representation on policy outcomes has been more consistent. Meier and Stewart's (1992) analysis revealed that the presence of African-American street-level bureaucrats (e.g., schoolteachers) had a significant effect on policy outcomes favoring African-American students. Meier (1993a) later replicated these findings for Latinos. He also tested the hypothesis proposed by Frank Thompson (1976) and Lenneal Henderson (1979) that a critical mass of minority administrators is needed under some circumstances before active representation occurs. Meier (1993a) found evidence to support this supposition, suggesting that active representation is most likely when sufficient minority management-level employees are present.

In a similar approach, John Hindera (1993a) focused on African Americans and women in the EEOC. He found that as the employment of African Americans increased, charges filed on behalf of that group also increased. Hindera (1993b) later extended this research to include Hispanics and obtained similar results.

Design of the Study

Two aspects of previous empirical research prompt the current study. First, few scholars have examined the link between passive and active representation. The positive relationship found in the literature between minority employment and policy outcomes favoring minority interests supports the basic assumptions of representative bureaucracy, but organizational settings examined have been limited to the EEOC and educational bureaucracies. To generalize these findings, this relationship warrants further examination in other policy settings. Second, no study has empirically tested a comprehensive model of representative bureaucracy. That is, no empirical research has examined the relationships between demographic characteristics, attitudes, and behaviors controlling for other factors that have been suggested to facilitate or impede the process of active representation.

This research examines whether passive representation is linked to active representation in the Farmers Home Administration's (FmHA) Rural Housing Loans program. This program was selected for numerous reasons discussed more fully in Chapter 4, but, primarily, it was chosen because administrators are granted discretion over decisions that are important to women and minority communities, and data are available that will allow administrators to be identified with their decisions. In the FmHA Rural Housing Loans program, county supervisors are granted a great deal of discretion to determine who receives rural housing loans, and records are maintained regarding all loan decisions. Furthermore, the FmHA is an agency with a reputation and record of poorly integrating women and minorities into its work force and implementing programs that adversely impact minorities (Baldwin 1968; Davidson 1987; Good 1968; Jones 1994; Martin 1985; Myrdal 1969; U.S. Commission on Civil Rights 1965, 1979, 1982). If the theory of representative bureaucracy garners empirical support in the FmHA, then one might reasonably expect it to operate in other governmental organizations with cultures and historical patterns of behavior less antagonistic to minority interests.

The first part of the analysis undertaken in this study examines variations in employment representation in FmHA districts. FmHA employment is modeled as a function of demographic, economic, organizational, and political factors. Next, the research turns to the linkage between passive and active representation in FmHA districts. The central question examined here is whether districts that employ more African Americans, Hispanics, Asian Americans, Native Americans, and women award more rural housing loans to these groups, controlling for demand and political factors.

In order to gain further insight into the potential of representative bureaucracy for increasing administrative responsiveness to the public, the research further examines the connection between the employment of racial and ethnic minorities in government agencies and the achievement of policy outcomes reflecting minority interests. The key concept in the model developed in Chapter 6 is the "minority representative role," thought to mediate between the demographic characteristics of agency administrators and policy outputs. In contrast to the bulk of research on representative bureaucracy, which focuses on components of the theory such as the relationship between backgrounds and attitudes or backgrounds and policy outputs, this research tests a model that suggests how the representative role develops and how it is reflected in administrative decisions.

In order to address these issues, information was collected from the FmHA, Bureau of the Census, and FmHA county supervisors. The Farmers Home Administration Freedom of Information Office provided fiscal years 1993 and 1994 data on the number of rural housing loan eligibility decisions made in each county office and personnel data. Supplementary information about the counties in which the FmHA field offices are located came from the 1990 U.S. Census. A mail survey was conducted of Farmers Home Administration county supervisors in the southern region of the United States.[2] The survey queried the FmHA county supervisors concerning their background, professional and community involvement, job activities, role expectations, and role perceptions. Responses were received from 234 individuals, or 61 percent of the sample. Of this group, 184 had complete data on the items included in the analysis.

Organization of the Book

Chapter 2 focuses on the dilemma of administrative responsibility and outlines the problems that representative bureaucracy may help to solve. Chapter 3 examines more closely the foci and trends in the representative bureaucracy literature with particular attention to research linking passive and active representation.

Chapter 4 introduces the FmHA and explains why it is a suitable environment for testing the concept of representative bureaucracy. Chapter 5 examines the process of passive representation and its subsequent impact on policy outcomes in FmHA districts. Chapter 6 sets forth a more comprehensive framework for examining representative bureaucracy. It explores the potential for "representative bureaucracy" by examining the linkages hypothesized between demographic representation, the assumption of a minority representative role on the part of public administrators, and the realization of policy outputs consistent with minority interests. Chapter 7 provides a summary of the findings and highlights theoretical and substantive implications.

Notes

1. For an excellent discussion of the difficulties associated with program implementation, see Mazmanian and Sabatier (1989).

2. Supervisors in the following states were surveyed: Alabama, Arkansas, Georgia, Kentucky, Louisiana, Mississippi, North Carolina, South Carolina, Tennessee, and Texas. The initial mailing included a questionnaire, cover letter, and postage-paid return envelope. Two weeks after following the initial mailing, a follow-up letter was mailed to respondents; a final reminder letter was sent three weeks after the follow-up.

2

Bureaucratic Power and the Dilemma of Administrative Responsibility

A critical and recurring question in the field of public administration is whether or not bureaucratic power is legitimate in terms of democratic constitutional values (Rosenbloom 1993). According to David H. Rosenbloom (1993, 482), legitimacy in this context is defined as "the population's belief that public administrators have a right to help make and implement public policy and to exercise political authority and discretion." If bureaucrats are not subject to direct popular control, can bureaucratic policy making be considered "democratic?" How can responsiveness to public interests and desires be assured in organizations that are not controlled by the public?

It does not appear that scholars will reach a consensus on these issues in the near future. Students of public administration generally agree, however, that government bureaucracies have enormous political power and that elected officials are unable to completely control them (Dodd and Schott 1979; Meier 1993b; Rourke 1992).[1] Thus, we are faced with the persistent problem of how best to ensure bureaucratic responsiveness and accountability to the people. The crux of this dilemma stems from the fact that bureaucrats exercise discretion in decision making. That is, civil servants have considerable latitude in determining the direction of programs and the nature, amount, and quality of benefits and sanctions provided by their agencies (Lipsky 1980).

Bureaucratic Discretion

In today's administrative state, bureaucrats have become policy makers in their own right, often granted complete autonomy as they exercise discretionary authority accorded to them by the legislature and executive (Shumavon and Hibbeln 1986). Congress has neither the time nor the resources to legislate in detail the rules and regulations for each program it authorizes. Typically, these responsibilities are delegated to specific agencies, which develop administrative rules and procedures to govern the manner in which the law is implemented. By adapting agency guidelines to the specific local environments they encounter, street-level bureaucrats exercise considerable additional influence on policy outcomes (Bryner 1987; Lipsky 1980; Mazmanian and Sabatier 1989; Prottas 1979; Scott 1997).

In the exercise of discretionary authority, upper-level officials are likely to shape the broad goals and direction of programs, while officials lower in the organization will influence the day-to-day operation and implementation of programs. For example, the federal government grants individual states the authority to establish eligibility standards for AFDC programs. Upper-level state agency officials establish the formal eligibility criteria and then delegate the authority to implement the program to local welfare offices. Local offices are responsible for receiving applications, determining who is eligible for the program, and providing services to clients. The quality of service (for instance, how long an individual must wait before being helped or how helpful the social worker is) is affected by the local social worker's caseload and attitude. Jeffrey Prottas (1979) found that intake social workers often have information that would facilitate an applicant's ability to navigate the bureaucratic maze, but in some cases the worker may not be required to provide that information to the applicant. Whether or not the social worker elects to share information with a client illustrates one way in which civil servants can facilitate or impede access to a public service.

The impact of bureaucratic discretion can also be seen in agencies such as the Federal Trade Commission (FTC), which has the ability to choose those firms or industries it may wish to investigate (Katzmann 1980). Similarly, inspectors from the Occupational Safety and Health Administration (OSHA) have latitude in deciding whether to fine an offending firm or to give it time to correct the problem. And, of course, individual police officers decide whom to arrest and whose behavior to overlook (Lipsky 1980). A number of decisions by public administrators have to be made at once, and often general rules give little guidance as to how decisions should be made (Hawkins and Manning forthcoming). It may be impossible or undesirable to write agency rules and procedures that will speak to all contingencies. Furthermore, it is not feasible to take into account an individual's special or unique circumstances without granting some degree of discretion within the rules. If general rules were constructed to govern all decisions, it would mean that individual circumstances would not be considered. Factors that may be important in specific cases would have to be ignored, and to do so might cause injustice to the individual as well as undermine the broad objectives of the program or agency. According to Kenneth C. Davis (1969, 15), "the justification for discretion is often the need for individual justice."

This problem is perhaps best illustrated with the exercise of police discretion. Police officers must often impose authority on people who are unpredictable, anxious, and frequently hostile. Many times when a police officer responds to a call, he or she can expect to encounter a situation with significant repercussions that requires the exercise of personal judgment involving frightened, intoxicated, drugged, angry, injured, or violent citizens. The officer must take charge of the situation and make fundamental decisions given the law, administrative rules, past training, and his or her personal experience. It is not feasible for a legislative body or the police department manual to identify all possible scenarios involving domestic violence, for example, and to prescribe the appropriate reaction to each. The best solution is to train officers to assess a situation and react accordingly.

The degree of discretion afforded to agencies is often used as an indicator of bureaucratic power. In addition to power that emanates from congressional and executive actions, agencies can mobilize other resources to influence and determine public policy. For example, agencies are able to use their alliances with clients both to influence congressional action and to protect themselves from it. In 1995, Medicare clients marshaled forces that lobbied to defeat the proposed Medicare reform. The ability of Congress and the president to control the bureaucracy is attenuated by bureaucratic power. Agencies with more power are typically better able to maneuver within the political process and less susceptible to legislative and executive control. Certainly there a number of factors that can contribute to bureaucratic power, and some of them are articulated in the following section (Hill 1992; Meier 1993b; Rainey 1991; Rourke 1992).

Sources of Bureaucratic Power

Scholars have debated how to define and measure bureaucratic power for years (Meier 1980, 1993b; Rainey 1991; Rourke 1992). For example, Kenneth J. Meier (1993c, 13) argues that "administrative power is the ability of a bureaucracy to allocate scarce societal resources." That is, bureaucrats exercise political power in determining who gets what, when, and how. Eugene Lewis (1980, 4) offers a more general definition of bureaucratic power: Bureaucracies are politically powerful because they exercise considerable influence and control over the formulation and implementation of policies. Similarly, Francis E. Rourke (1992, 1) broadly conceives of bureaucratic power as the influence of administrative agencies in the policy process.

Despite the difficulties of providing a precise definition of bureaucratic power, scholars have reached some consensus on important determinants of bureaucratic power.[2] Larry Hill (1992) succinctly reviews many of these sources. His synthesis of the literature provides insight into factors that contribute to the growing influence of government bureaucracies in the United States (see Table 2.1). Overall, sources of power are grouped into two categories, those inherent in the nature of bureaucracy, and those related to the nature of American politics. The following discussion expands upon the framework of bureaucratic power proposed by Hill (1992).

Power Inherent in the Nature of Bureaucracy

Power inherent in bureaucratic structure is ultimately derived from four sources: legal resources, material and other resources, organizational resources, and agency cohesion.

Legal Resources

The law, for example, provides the basis for the bureaucracy's existence, delineates its powers and jurisdictions, and legitimates the enforcement of decisions by the bureaucracy. Marshall Dimock (1980, 31) wrote:

> To the public administrator, law is something very positive and concrete. It is his authority. The term he customarily uses to describe it is

Table 2.1

Sources of Bureaucratic Power

Inherent in the Nature of Bureaucracy

Legal	Basis of existence; delineates powers & jurisdictions; legitimates enforcement
Material and other	Monetary and nonmonetary rewards; capital resources (automobiles, buildings, supplies, computers)
Organizational	Monopolistic nature of service provision; specialization of bureaucracy; extent and nature of expertise; leadership
Cohesion	Agency cohesion (recruiting, hiring, promotion strategies, training, agency socialization, administrative rules)

Peculiar to the Nature of American Politics

Fragmented & multiple sources of control	General public, attentive public (clients, interest groups, media); legislature (subcommittees); executive (presidential support, staff agencies)
Latitude in policy process	Discretion; Implementation

Source: Adapted from Hill (1992).

"my mandate." It is "his" law, something he feels a proprietary interest in. It does three things: tells him what the legislature expects him to accomplish, fixes limits to his authority, and sets forth the substantive and procedural rights of the individual and group. Having a positive view of his mandate, the administrator considers himself both an interpreter and a builder. He is a builder because every time he applies old law to new situations he builds the law. Therefore, law, like administration, is government in action.

Statutes, executive orders, and court decisions provide bureaucrats legal authority or legitimate power in the policy process, as well as outline the structure that guides a mandate's implementation (French and Raven 1959; Hill 1992; Long 1949; Mazmanian and Sabatier 1989). The extent to which legal objectives are ambiguous, formal decision rules are stipulated, and the system is loosely or poorly integrative will determine the degree of latitude granted to implementing agencies (Goggin, Bowman, Lester, and O'Toole 1990; Mazmanian and Sabatier 1989). Statutes and executive orders can substantially affect the extent of power wielded by an agency by granting it both legitimacy and discretion in the policy process.

Material and Other Resources

It is also the case that bureaucratic power is derived from access to material resources (Meier 1980). John R.P. French, Jr., and Bertram Raven (1959), in their classic typology of the bases for social power, refer to this as reward-based power. Bureaucrats manage large budgets, buildings, and other supplies and have access to computers and other high-tech equipment. They also allocate services, goods, money, prestige, privileges, and other perks to clients, employees, and suppliers. Such resources may entice individuals to support certain agencies if they think those agencies are likely to spend money in ways that will benefit them directly or indirectly. This is illustrated by the Small Business Administration (SBA), which is authorized to finance start-up and expansion costs of small businesses and to provide other services, such as marketing consultation, for small business owners. As a result, self-interest may motivate small business owners to support the SBA. As long as clients, employees, and suppliers are dependent on these agency resources, they are likely to comply with the agency. However, this form of power is effective only as long as the resources are available and the groups are dependent on them (Hargrove and Glidewell 1990).

Organizational Resources

Organizational resources such as the monopolistic nature of service provision, the specialization of bureaucracies, the extent and nature of expertise, and agency leadership are also fundamental determinants of agency power (Hill 1992). As mentioned above, the degree to which others depend on an agency's resources has an impact on an agency's power. Often, government provides goods and services that are not offered by other organizations (Rourke 1992). Individuals do not necessarily have other options and subsequently are highly dependent on the agency providing the good or service. For example, the only entity that issues passports to U.S. citizens is the United States Department of State. Similarly, the U.S. Postal Service is utilized by most citizens to deliver and distribute their mail because they lack other affordable options.

In addition, power accrues to agency units that manage contingencies or parts of an organization's operations that are critical (Rainey 1991). "Units that handle the biggest problems facing the organization gain power" (Rainey 1991, 76). Similarly, agencies that are responsible for goods and services crucial to the government, such as the Department of Defense with its role in maintaining national security, are likely to be more powerful than those perceived by the public as less important, such as National Railroad Passenger Corporation (Amtrak).

Specialization and expertise also confer bureaucratic power through superior knowledge of a problem or policy area. Bureaucracies have several advantages over other political institutions in developing superior policy information. The size of bureaucracy, for instance, permits specialization beyond what political institutions are capable of developing. Large public organizations have the manpower to divide complex problems and issues into smaller and more manageable tasks (Rourke 1992). Bureaucrats acquire expertise by concentrating on these tasks over time. Legislatures and citizens, on the other hand, are at a disadvantage, in that they only address issues serially when they become politically important (Lewis 1980). As Meier (1993b, 54) has observed, "specialization allows bureaucracy as an entity to know more about a public policy than any individual or institution that lacks its size, continuity, and permanence." Specialization results in bureaucracies producing and controlling more detailed information regarding specific policy issues than other institutions (Lewis 1980; Berry in Meier 1993b). The United States Department of Agriculture (USDA), for example, conducts a variety of agricultural service functions producing more detailed reports and research on agricultural issues than any other institution (Stillman 1992).

The presence of professionally trained administrators suggests that political leaders will be given competent technical advice and that programs will be implemented by skilled specialists. The increasing number of professionals employed by agencies adds to the credibility of policy advice issued by bureaucracies and subsequently influences how that advice is received by elected officials and citizens (Hargrove and Glidewell 1990; Meier 1993b; Rainey 1991; Rourke 1992). Furthermore, the type of professionals employed by an agency influences elected officials and citizens' perceptions of the agency (Hargrove and Glidewell 1990). Professionals or experts in highly technical and scientific arenas, such as AIDS research, are highly regarded by nonprofessionals who typically defer to the "expert's advice." For example, the National Institutes of Health (NIH) is dominated by individuals with highly professionalized training in the fields of medicine and science. As a result, NIH is granted considerable independence in its operations and is expected to provide solutions to the most complex and critical medical problems in the United States. Agencies employing large shares of revered professionals, such as NIH, are likely to accrue power. On the other hand, agencies employing professional experts in less respected fields, such as social services, are less likely to be politically powerful (Hargrove and Glidewell 1990).

Given the number of professionals specializing and focusing on particular policy issues, bureaucracies should produce better, more effective policies over time (Meier 1993b). According to Lewis (1980, 6), specialization and expertise "inevitably entail some loss of autonomy for the formal policy makers who are usually found in legislatures, among elected executives, and . . . in the courts."

Organizational leadership can also affect agency power. Agencies are sometimes led by individuals who seek to expand the organization's goals, mandates, functions, and power (Lewis 1980). Leaders can build agency power both internally and externally. Internally, an agency leader can create an organizational culture that motivates personnel and promotes expertise (Meier 1993b). Externally, leaders can increase agency influence in the policy process by developing and nourishing external constituencies, such as congressional members, interest groups, and clients, to support agency goals and programs (Doig and Hargrove 1987). J. Edgar Hoover serves as an excellent example of a leader who dramatically increased agency power (Lewis 1980). Hoover transformed the Federal Bureau of Investigation (FBI) from a "minor, corrupt, and thoroughly inefficient and ineffective investigatory agency into a colossus that rose to dominate its putative superiors, just as the proverbial, perverse tail wags the superfluous dog" (Lewis 1980, 228).

Cohesion Within the Agency

The final source of power inherent in bureaucratic structure, presented in Table 2.1, pertains to agency cohesion. Agencies can, for example, structure organizational practices to achieve internal cohesion. Cohesion has been defined as the commitment of employees to the agency's goals and objectives (Meier 1993b). An agency dominated by individuals who believe in its goals will be better able to motivate its members (Meier 1993b). By recruiting and hiring new employees who are committed to those missions, agency leaders create an organizational culture that is supportive of specific goals and agendas. Furthermore, agencies can utilize administrative rules, training, and other socialization techniques to promote internal cohesion. Meier (1993b) believes that one of the best examples of agency cohesion is exemplified by the Peace Corps. In the 1960s, a large number of top university graduates elected to enter the Peace Corps rather than taking well-paying jobs (Meier 1993b).

The extent of power wielded by an agency is partly determined by the factors discussed; however, other conditions and factors also affect bureaucratic power. Agencies may increase their influence by mobilizing support of different political and nonpolitical actors in the policy process.

American Politics and Bureaucratic Power

Fragmented and Multiple Sources of Control

The nature of American politics contributes to bureaucratic power. Hill (1992) argues that a bureaucracy's base of power is enhanced because it faces fragmented and multiple sources of control. Bureaucracies can garner political support and opposition from different institutions and constituents to support their internal platforms or to curb political opposition. Administrative agencies can draw political support from three main sources: the public, the legislature, and the executive office. Agencies may utilize all of these sources simultaneously or may emphasize one to the exclusion of the others. Often, agencies have to balance one source against another.

Agencies need support both from the general public and from attentive publics such as clients and interest groups (Rainey 1991; Rourke 1992). Some agencies will receive public support or opposition solely based on the dominant values and beliefs of the organization or the social construction of their clients (Rainey 1991; Rourke 1992; Schneider and Ingram 1993). For example, the Federal Emergency Management Agency (FEMA) and the Department of Defense usually receive public support because citizens value personal and national security. Erwin C. Hargrove and John Glidewell (1990) argue that some public administrators have impossible jobs because the public perceives their clients as "irresponsible, strange, lazy, or antisocial," while other administrators' jobs are more respected because they serve responsible, diligent clients, such as veterans.

Public support for an agency may be cultivated, in part, by the agency's fostering a generally favorable public attitude toward itself (Rainey 1991). For example, some agencies, such as the U.S. Army, may seek to advertise their accomplishments. The Army focuses its efforts on recruitment and uses a variety of media, such as newspapers, billboards, and television, to advertise. The Golden Knights, the Army's parachute display team, also travel throughout the United States participating in air shows as part of this effort. Similarly, the Air Force's Thunderbirds and the Navy's Blue Angels are used to promote Air Force and Navy recruitment. Other agencies receive widespread public attention for certain projects they administer, such as the National Aeronautics and Space Administration (NASA) when it launches a space shuttle. Of course, a disaster such as the 1986 *Challenger* catastrophe can have a devastating effect on the public's perception of an organization's ability to perform.

An agency can also draw considerable support from those individuals who benefit from programs it administers (clients). This is illustrated by the Department of Veterans Affairs (VA), which operates programs that benefit veterans and their families. The VA's clientele is a cohesive and visible group as they share the bond of either having participated in military organizations or having had family members who have been involved in the military. As a whole, veterans and their families provide substantial backing for the VA and wield considerable influence in the policy process. Similarly, the Administration on Aging, as the lead agency within the Department of Health and Human Services on all issues concerning aging, serves the needs and interests of elderly citizens and in return receives their support.

Agencies may serve also as advocates for groups and therefore ensure that these groups are not overlooked when decisions are being made. Interest groups employ thousands of individuals who advise the federal government on their own behalf (Levine, Peters, and Thompson 1990). Administrators may use interest groups to promote their own preferences, but power flows in the opposite direction as well.

The American Medical Association (AMA) is one of the most power-ful interest groups in Washington, D.C. This power became evident recently as the AMA played a pivotal role in killing the Clinton administration's plan for health care reform.

The amount of power and autonomy derived from clientele and interest groups varies depending on their size, cohesiveness, and ability to mobilize. The literature suggests that agencies with larger clienteles will receive a larger share of the benefits distributed by Congress (Meier 1993b; Rourke 1992). According to Rainey (1991, 56), "the most effective support comes from well-organized, cohesive groups, strongly committed to the agency and its programs." Clients and inter-est groups have the opportunity to define their interests, organize them-selves, persuade others to support their cause, gain access to elected officials, and influence political agendas. A group that can mobilize its members in such ways is likely to increase an agency's power in the policy process.

Bureaucratic power may also be influenced by other members of an issue network, such as journalists, congressional staff members, and executive staff members. Media coverage plays an important role in governance (Rainey 1991). For example, newspapers and broadcast news often cover stories about the misconduct of public officials and agencies. Although both of these news outlets report illegal or wasteful activity in both the private and public sectors, a majority of the stories focus on government agencies. A recent survey of articles in thirty major newspapers over a seven-year period revealed that 70 percent of the whistleblowing incidents receiving news coverage occurred in the public sector (Brewer 1995). Negative press can damage the reputation of an agency or public official, which could result in further public scrutiny, more congressional and executive oversight, reduced pro-gram budgets, and personnel cuts (Rainey 1991).

Agencies can gather support from the legislature both formally and informally. The formal authority of Congress to write legislation, ap-propriate funds, and oversee agency operations has an impact on bu-reaucratic power. Agencies are dependent on Congress to pass legislation to authorize, extend, or expand programs. As mentioned previously, many of the directives issued by Congress are vague and grant considerable discretion to agencies. However, sometimes legisla-tors write detailed and precise mandates that do not allow administra-tors to exercise discretion (Rainey 1991). The degree of discretion granted to an agency has a significant impact on its power in the policy process.

Congress also controls the final appropriations decisions (Rainey 1991; Wildavsky 1988). The annual appropriations process causes agencies to be dependent upon Congress for budget allocations and to justify themselves yearly or risk losing funding (Wildavsky 1988). According to Rourke (1992, 66), "no matter how broad an agency's formal authority, its real power turns ultimately upon its fiscal resources." The extent and quality of services as well as enforcement strategies are determined by the amount of money an agency is allocated to spend (Rourke 1992).

Legislative bodies also oversee agency operations. They frequently conduct hearings, and oversee audits and investigations of particular agencies (Rainey 1991). Members of Congress can request oversight agencies, such as the U.S. General Accounting Office (GAO), to conduct program audits and investigations. The information obtained during these events may be critical in determining whether to eliminate, continue, or expand a program. Similarly, legislative committees oversee agencies, conduct hearings, and develop legislation relating to them (Rainey 1991). These committees have a large degree of control over what legislation reaches the floor and what aspects of the agency will be formally evaluated. As a result, a committee can shape significantly the policy initiatives and direction of agencies it oversees (Wildavsky 1988).

It is vital that agencies establish good relationships with legislators on key committees, especially if they are not strongly supported by the public. Although forging relationships with legislative committees and subcommittees is eased since congressmen tend to be placed on committees and subcommittees in which they have a vested interest, agency leaders can play a critical role in cultivating these relationships (Doig and Hargrove 1987; Meier 1993b; Wildavsky 1988). Members of Congress also have a great deal to gain by protecting agencies that serve their constituents (Moe 1987; Weingast and Moran 1983). Moreover, interest groups may encourage attention to certain agencies, according to Aaron Wildavsky (1988), with campaign assistance and other forms of support. Over time, a mutually supportive relationship among committee members, interest groups, and agencies develops. These alliances have been called "iron triangles," and the strength of these triangles varies widely (Wildavsky 1988). Stronger alliances are likely to lead to greater agency power.

Finally, agencies may derive support from the executive branch. Meier (1993b) noted that the best political support in the executive branch is presidential support. For example, President Reagan's support for national defense resulted in dramatically higher expenditures for military programs (Meier 1993b). Agencies may also obtain support from staff agencies of the executive branch, such as the Office of Management and Budget (OMB), the Office of Personnel Management (OPM), and the General Services Administration (GSA), all of which have partial control over operational resources (Meier 1993b; Rourke 1992). OMB plays a critical role in the appropriations process; OPM influences recruitment, retention, and promotion of agency personnel; and GSA oversees the purchase, operation, and upkeep of federal buildings.

Latitude in the Policy Process

The latitude granted to agencies and administrators in the policy process contributes significantly to bureaucratic power, as we have seen. Although the inherent power of implementation is a key to bureaucracies' political power (Meier 1993b), agency involvement extends beyond executing the will of elected officials. Agencies also participate in other areas of the policy process, including agenda setting, formulation, adoption, and evaluation. By working closely with elected officials at various stages of the policy process, administrators are linked intimately with their decisions. Even internal decisions within public agencies are inherently political because they involve the allocation of public monies and resources. It is a fallacy, therefore, to portray administrative questions as distinct from political questions.

Agencies are actors in the political process and their decisions are political decisions. Although the degree of power varies among agencies, the fact remains that bureaucrats exercise a great deal of influence in the policy process. Power accrues to agencies that manage critical agency operations, employ technically trained administrators, have charismatic leadership, have highly committed work forces, and have political support from the public, the legislature, and the executive.

Elected officials have formal authority that can be used to limit bureaucratic power, but other forces, such as strong public support, agency reputation, and bureaucratic expertise, may complicate political decisions and result in grants of autonomy to agencies. Since bureaucrats are not elected by the public, and thereby not directly accountable to them, how do we ensure that bureaucratic power does not threaten democratic principles? In order to address this issue, the following discussion begins with a brief historical overview of the tension between bureaucratic power and democratic theory.

Reconciling the Tension

In the era 1829–1883, when party loyalty was the primary prerequisite for public office and the bureaucracy was considered an extension of the party in power, the conflict between administrative power and democratic theory may have been less of a problem. Theoretically, politically appointed civil servants shared the party's political values and, more importantly, they were directly accountable and responsible to the elected officials who appointed them. The electorate, in turn, could hold both the elected officials and civil servants accountable at the polls (Ingraham and Rosenbloom 1990). However, the creation of a merit-based civil service in the late nineteenth century raised new questions because the requisites for public office shifted from party loyalty and accountability to merit and political neutrality. It was soon after that point that the literature on public administration began to emerge and the issue of bureaucratic power became a central concern in scholarly writing.

Reconciling the Dilemma:
The Politics–Administration Dichotomy

The earliest scholarship in public administration proposed a dichotomy between politics and administration (Goodnow 1900; Wilson 1887) that continues to influence the structure and organization of public agencies today. Under the dichotomy, bureaucrats were not considered political actors and did not wield political power in the policy process. Instead, they were responsible for implementing, in the most efficient way, political mandates and directives as specified by elected officials. Because civil servants were viewed as apolitical technocrats of the state, bureaucratic power was not perceived as a significant problem. Woodrow Wilson (1887, 11) argued that

> administration lies outside the proper sphere of politics. Administrative questions are not political questions. Although politics sets the tasks for administration, it should not be suffered to manipulate its offices.

Wilson drew a distinction between what ought to be in the political sphere and what ought to be in the nonpartisan/nonpolitical administrative sphere. Frank Goodnow's (1900) book, *Politics and Administration*, moved beyond Wilson's dialogue on partisan politics by arguing that administrators do not make political decisions. Goodnow (1900, 27) stated that "politics has to do with the guidance or influencing of governmental policy, while administration has to do with the execution of that policy." William Willoughby (1919) also declared that the bureaucracy was responsible for "putting into effect . . . policies as determined by other [political] organs." Clearly, as the academic field of public administration was emerging, scholars believed that administrative questions were distinguishable from political questions.

In addition, the adoption of private sector principles to public sector organizations was emphasized in the early 1900s. Frederick Taylor (1911) contended that managers could carefully observe daily tasks and identify the most efficient way of completing those tasks. Because of the time and motion studies Taylor (1911) conducted, he is often championed as the father of the scientific management movement. Scientific management techniques were employed in the public sector to enhance the status of management and to improve the efficiency and effectiveness of service delivery (Ingraham and Rosenbloom 1990).

A core value underlying these early approaches was efficiency. Willoughby (1927) asserted that organizational efficiency could be improved because scientific principles of public administration existed, and administrators would be experts if they learned how to apply these principles. This approach was further advocated in the Brownlow Committee's report and Luther Gulick's and Lydall Urwick's (1937) essays on the principles of administration. Both of these works emphasized methods of strengthening presidential control over the bureaucracy. Gulick's article, "Notes on the Science of Administration," (Gulick and Urwick 1937) is often cited as the most influential statement of the administrative principles approach (Levine, Peters, and Thompson 1990). During this period, scholars believed that a "science of management" existed that would enable the bureaucracy to act on the basis of objectively established nonpolitical principles (Gulick and Urwick 1937; Taylor 1911).

At this time, scholars did not perceive problems of administrative power and the dilemma of accountability so long as a dichotomy between politics and administration was asserted (Ingraham and

Rosenbloom 1990). Elected officials, who were directly accountable to the people, were responsible for rendering political decisions. Administrators were responsible only for efficiently executing the will of elected officials to whom they were directly accountable. The fact that administrators were at least three steps removed from the electorate was not an issue because, from this perspective, administrators were not involved in political decision making.

The Fallacy of the Politics–Administration Dichotomy

While the politics–administration dichotomy created an acceptable niche for the bureaucracy in the American political arena, it nevertheless failed to coincide with reality. The principles of administration proved to be little more than proverbs, and politics and administration, it was soon learned, were inextricably entwined (Dahl 1947; Simon 1947). In the following paragraph, Allen Schick (1975) captures the impact of this realization on the field of public administration:

> The destruction of the dichotomy also destroyed the unifying ethic of public administration and rendered it impotent to integrate political realities into its core values. The political shock was damaging because the pluralist norms were sharply at variance with classic administrative ideals. In place of form and order, there was muddling through and the babble of competing interests. Hierarchy gave way to bargaining, rationality to group demands. (Schick 1975, 160)

The new realism about administrative life and the increasing awareness of the power of government bureaucracies sharpened scholars' and political actors' sensitivity to issues of accountability, responsibility, and responsiveness of public organizations (Fesler 1975). These three terms are often used interchangeably; however, the terms both differ and overlap in meaning. Accountability implies that civil servants must answer to elected officials (Levine, Peters, and Thompson 1990). Responsibility, on the other hand, is often divided into two schools of thought on the role of bureaucracy in democratic society (Saltzstein 1985). Some scholars contend that civil servants are legally or ethically accountable to elected officials, while others assert that public administrators should be responsible to the public (Gilbert 1959; Saltzstein 1985). Grace Hall Saltzstein (1985) argued that each view of administrative responsibility leads to different notions of administrative responsiveness. The boundaries of the concept can be identified by answering the questions of responsiveness "to whom?" "to what?" and "in what form?"

Over the years, scholars have proposed a number of concepts, perspectives, and theories to control, justify, or legitimate bureaucratic power.[3] Various approaches have emphasized legislative oversight and executive control, judicial review of administrative decisions, methods of increasing public access to bureaucratic decision-making processes, and the inculcation of administrative ethics (Frederickson 1993; Gilbert 1959; Kaufman 1956; Meier 1993b; Ostrom 1973; Redford 1969; Rohr 1986; Waldo 1980). Each approach differs from the others in its view of administrative responsibility. Two of these theories are sketched below to illustrate different perspectives on bureaucratic responsibility and roles.[4]

The New Public Administration and an Emphasis on Equity

In the late 1960s, a new perspective called the *new public administration* emerged from a gathering of public administration scholars who convened at the Minnowbrook conference site of Syracuse University in September of 1968 to discuss the current state and future of the field of public administration. The conference was held during the Vietnam War, the movement for equal rights of minorities, and the war on poverty (Waldo 1971). Scholars generally agreed that as society's chosen instrument for dealing with its problems, public administration needed to adapt to the changing and turbulent environment (Waldo 1971).

Scholars hold somewhat different opinions about what new public administration intended, and it is difficult to present a coherent and concise discussion of the concept.[5] Typically, however, much of the dialogue centers on George Frederickson's emphasis on social equity.[6] New public administration supporters accept that administrators are not value-neutral decision makers and that they maximize their own values when making decisions (Frederickson 1976). Given that we accept the above assumption, we have to decide *what* values we want public administrators to maximize. Frederickson (1971) contended that values underlying traditional public administration theories, such as efficiency, effectiveness, accountability to elected officials, and political nonpartisanship, were not wrong but incomplete. Frederickson (1971) suggested that administrators should value more than neutrality and efficiency. In fact, they should be committed to values that promote both good management and social equity. As an approach, new public administration sought both to promote policies that would improve the quality of life for all citizens (Frederickson 1971) and to ensure bureaucratic responsibility to citizens.

Public Choice as an Alternative Paradigm
for Public Administration

Shortly thereafter, a very different school of thought about public administration took root. Vincent Ostrom's *The Intellectual Crisis in Public Administration* was published in 1973 at the time the Watergate scandal was unfolding and the Nixon presidency was falling apart (Sherwood 1990). Here Ostrom outlined problems in the field of public administration and offered the theory of public choice as an alternative paradigm for the field.

James M. Buchanan, one of the leading scholars in public choice theory, characterized public choice as follows:

> The critically important bridge between the behavior of persons who act in the marketplace and the behavior of persons who act in the political process must be analyzed. The "theory of public choice" can be interpreted as the construction of such a bridge. The approach requires only the simple assumption that the same individuals act in both relationships. (1972, 12)

Public choice theory assumes that all actors in the political arena, such as voters, elected officials, interest groups, clients, and bureaucrats, seek to maximize their own self-interest. According to this view, public administrators act on behalf of their interests rather than automatically translating law or the public interest into public policy (Niskanen 1971). Similarly, citizens are viewed as consumers who will rationally apply their preferences in evaluating goods and services (Ostrom 1973).

Ostrom contended that government provision of goods and services is not the only means of meeting the needs and preferences of citizens (Ostrom 1973). He suggested that scholars should consider two central questions regarding the production of public goods and services: First, should the government be providing a service or good? Second, how should services or goods be produced?

Under certain conditions, public choice theory suggests that fragmented and overlapping delivery are an effective means of rendering goods and services. Since individuals are self-interested and deliberate in decision making, they will select from a set of alternative delivery methods based on their preferences (Ostrom 1973). Charles H. Levine, B. Guy Peters, and Frank J. Thompson (1990, 287) summarized this school of thought:

> To public choice theorists, the success of the orthodox prescriptions for hierarchical arrangements, clear lines of authority, technical proficiency, and political neutrality has meant "large, distant, and unresponsive bureaucracies; inefficient and ineffective public programs; and unrealistic expectations about the abilities of elected chief executives." To remedy these ills, public choice advocates have proposed major and sometimes radical changes in the structure and processes of public administration.

For example, public choice supporters recommend creating market-like arrangements, such as contracting out for public goods and services, implementing user fees and voucher systems, and adopting co-production strategies. Furthermore, citizens are able to exercise some control over bureaucracies through their choices. Using alternative service delivery options and increasing citizen control may reduce an agency's power.

This brief introduction of two alternative paradigms for the field of public administration—new public administration and public choice—demonstrates that scholars hold very different opinions about the appropriate role of public bureaucracies. New public administration proposes that administrators balance more traditional bureaucratic values with values often absent in the political process, such as social equity. The approach assumes that administrators are motivated by a fundamental concern for social equity that guides their decisions. New public administration has evolved into a broader agenda for social change. Recent issues embraced by this movement include affirmative action and improved accommodations for the disabled. In the case of affirmative action, the controversy over discrimination and reverse discrimination illustrates how social equity can conflict with other goals, such as efficiency (Okun 1975). In contrast, the public choice movement assumes that bureaucrats are self-interested actors. They are not responsible for discerning and protecting particular needs of citizens; instead they view citizens as consumers who will express their preferences through their choices (Niskanen 1971). Public choice champions economic efficiency through bureaucratic decentralization and alternative modes of service delivery. One current application drawing on such principles is the use of vouchers for subsidizing low-income residential housing. Such programs typically grant housing vouchers to qualified, low-income citizens that can be applied toward the housing unit of their choice. Thus citizens are empowered to express their housing preferences as they are not limited solely to publicly owned or operated housing units. These two movements clearly illustrate different perspectives on public administration. These and other viewpoints on public administration encompass distinct positions on what public administrators should be responsible for and to whom administrators should be responsible (Ingraham and Rosenbloom 1990).

Perspectives on Bureaucratic Responsibility

Approaches proposed to control, justify, or legitimate bureaucratic power are typically founded on divergent assumptions about administrative responsibility. One orientation rests upon the assumption that agencies and bureaucrats are controlled by elected officials. The other assumes that administrators are attuned to and act on behalf of the citizenry (Saltzstein 1985, 289; 1992). Each view holds distinct implications for administrative behavior and action. Saltzstein (1992, 68) argues that the perspective on bureaucratic responsibility "becomes an important component of the bureaucrats' generalized role conceptions that—presumably—affect their behavior."

Responsiveness to Elected Officials

The first approach assumes that American society can maintain a bureaucracy that is responsive to the direction and control of elected officials. Bureaucratic power is palatable because the interests of the public are represented by elected officials, who in turn grant authority to the bureaucracy (Redford 1969). The politics–administration dichotomy and bureaucratic neutrality are founded upon this view of responsibility (Saltzstein 1985). Administrators are tasked with neutrally and efficiently implementing policies formulated by elected officials and are likely to "approach substantive responsiveness in terms of expertise or professionalism" (Saltzstein 1992, 69). Scholars studying congressional dominance and presidential control also assume that supremacy rests with elected officials (for example, Barke and Riker 1982; Calvert, McCubbins, and Weingast 1988; Cary 1967; Moe 1987; Weingast 1984; Weingast and Moran 1983, 1984). Elected officials are able to use direct and indirect mechanisms to exert control and influence over bureaucratic agents. For example, the president, with the approval of the Senate, selects political appointees to lead public agencies, who are in return responsible for ensuring that the president's political platform is incorporated into agencies' goals and practices. Ronald Reagan used Donald J. Devine, the appointed director of OPM, for instance, to assert his authority over the federal personnel system. Furthermore, congressmen are able to use an array of incentives and sanctions to induce agencies to behave in intended ways. Congress allocates resources and has formal oversight authority and can exercise it, for example, through new legislation, hearings, and prohibitive mandates (Weingast and Moran 1983). Scholars adhering to this framework view bureaucracy as a direct tool of elected officials. Thus, bureaucrats are expected to be responsive to elected officials, who provide representation of the people (Gilbert 1959; Redford 1969; Saltzstein 1985).

Responsiveness to the Public

A second orientation suggests that bureaucrats should be responsive directly to the public; however, little consensus has been reached over how the public's wishes should be incorporated into the process (Saltzstein 1985, 1992). One group of scholars has argued that the representative character of bureaucracy makes it potentially responsive to the needs and desires of the people (Krisolv 1974; Long 1952; Meier 1993b; Saltzstein 1985, 1992). A bureaucracy that is demographically diverse should increase access to and input from an increasing number of perspectives. As a result, it should deliver decisions and services that are more responsive to the populace. Other approaches have exhorted public administrators to pursue the public interest (see Marini 1971; Perry 1996; Perry and Wise 1990; Wamsley et al. 1990). For example, students of public service motivation suggest that civil servants internalize a unique public service ethic that makes them more likely to act in the public interest (Rainey 1982; Perry and Wise 1990; Wamsley et al. 1990). Public interest, however, is an elu-

Table 2.2

Gilbert's Framework of Administrative Responsibility

	Internal	External
Formal	Presidential controls	Congressional oversight; judiciary
Informal	Professionalism; ethics; representative work force	Public interest; interest groups; clients

Source: Gilbert (1959).

sive concept and thus administrators are left to develop their own opinions about what decisions and policies are in the public interest. They must rationally discern and weigh citizen needs, desires, and preferences to determine alternatives that approximate the will of the public. Under this framework, bureaucrats are expected to be responsive directly to the citizenry.

Charles E. Gilbert's Typology of Administrative Responsibility

In a detailed discussion of administrative responsibility, Charles E. Gilbert (1959) developed a two-by-two typology that divides administrative relationships into four categories: internal formal; internal informal; external formal; and external informal (see Table 2.2). The formal categories of responsibility focus on the relationship between elected officials and bureaucracy, whereas the informal positions address the direct link between bureaucracy and citizens.[7] The internal formal position stresses direction and control by the executive branch, such as the president's power to appoint loyal supporters to lead and operate agencies. The external formal position places reliance upon formal direction and control by Congress and the courts. For example, Congress can use sunset laws to increase control over a program by requiring reauthorization after a specified period of time, while the courts can intervene to influence bureaucratic procedures. The internal informal position refers to approaches emphasizing the ethical, representative, and professional aspects of public service as sources of responsibility. Finally, the external informal position embraces interest-group representation, citizen participation, and the relationship between organized groups and administrative agencies.

The debate between the informal and formal schools of administrative responsibility is illustrated in an often-cited discourse between Carl Friedrich (1940) and Herman Finer (1941). Friedrich (1940) contended that administrators face a dual standard of responsibility: technical expertise and public opinion. Thus, administrators have to balance objectivity and professionalism with public needs and wishes. Finer (1941, 336–337) countered that eventually "there is an abuse of power when external punitive controls are lacking." It is Congress's role and duty, according to Finer, to represent the public's wishes.

Given the nature and power of modern bureaucracy, the more formal means of ensuring administrative responsibility may be inadequate by themselves (Gilbert 1959). Despite the mechanisms of external political control, bureaucrats still exercise discretion in the policy implementation process. Judith Gruber (1987, 12) argued that "bureaucracies pose a problem for democracy when they make government decisions—that is, public policy—and thereby short electoral circuit channels of public control." Some scholars contend that it is not likely that the government will be "responsible" through the normal channels to voters of all races, genders, classes, and religions unless the bureaucracy is recruited on a broadly representative basis (Levitan 1946). Whether and to what extent the bureaucracy will be responsible may well depend on public administrators' values, attitudes, and beliefs (Kingsley 1944; Kranz 1976; Meier 1993c). Samuel Krislov and David H. Rosenbloom (1981, 22) contend that

> [i]t is not the power of public bureaucracies per se, but their unrepresentative power, that constitutes the greatest threat to democratic government. If this power cannot be constrained by legislators and political executives, it can nevertheless be made to operate democratically by making it representative of the public.

Representative Bureaucracy and Administrative Responsibility

Representative bureaucracy suggests that a bureaucracy that broadly reflects the interests, opinions, needs, desires, and values of the general public has legitimate authority in the policy process. A representative bureaucracy would help to ensure that the values and interests of all groups in society are articulated and hence brought to bear upon decisions made and policies formulated. The logic underlying the concept of representative bureaucracy is mapped in Figure 2.1. Demographic background characteristics are important because differences in demographic background are associated with differences in socialization experiences. Socialization experiences in turn influence and shape a person's values, attitudes, and beliefs. Because bureaucrats maximize their own values when making decisions, differences in values should produce differences in bureaucratic decisions. Thus, agencies should produce policy outputs that benefit the groups of people who are demographically represented.

Paul Van Riper (1958, 558) argued that "the concept of representative bureaucracy offers one of the few positive approaches toward a new theory of administrative responsibility and perhaps even of public administration in general." Although this approach was first introduced in the academic literature by J. Donald Kingsley in 1944, the movement toward a more representative bureaucracy in the United States dates back to the early 1800s. Between 1789 and 1828, the civil service was an extension of the ruling political elite (Van Riper 1958). Public servants were drawn from upper social and economic classes, and the standards for holding public office were fitness of character, competence, and loyalty to the Constitution. Fitness of character was measured by "family background, educational attainment, honor and esteem, and of, course, loyalty to the new government—all tempered by a sagacious regard for geographic representation" (Mosher 1982, 57). As a whole, the civil service did not mirror the social and economic composition of society. During this period, Thomas Jefferson was the only president to veer from this staffing strategy. Jefferson replaced approximately 15 percent of the public work force with politically loyal associates (Van Riper 1958). Although these replacements were marginally lower in social status, they still did not reflect the common man (Ingraham and Rosenbloom 1990).

The election of Andrew Jackson in 1829 marked a distinct shift in the form and direction of the civil service. The Jacksonian Revolution opened the way for the democratization of the political process by making the system more accessible to previously excluded segments of the population. Control of the bureaucracy was transferred from the self-appointed elite to a more representative population (Van Riper

Figure 2.1. **Logic of Representative Bureaucracy**

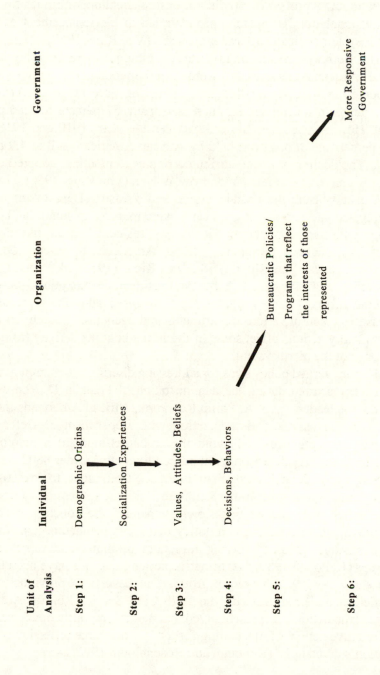

Unit of Analysis	Individual	Organization	Government
Step 1:	Demographic Origins		
Step 2:	Socialization Experiences		
Step 3:	Values, Attitudes, Beliefs		
Step 4:	Decisions, Behaviors		
Step 5:		Bureaucratic Policies/ Programs that reflect the interests of those represented	
Step 6:			More Responsive Government

1958). Although the spoils system led to greater representation, it was not without its problems and did not ensure equal opportunities for the entire population. Ultimately, scandals led to the replacement of the spoils system with a merit system in 1883 (Van Riper 1958).

The merit system was an important vehicle for increasing the number of African Americans and women in the federal civil service (Van Riper 1958). Between 1881 and 1910, the percentage of African Americans in federal service increased from .57 percent to 5.86 percent. However, progress slowed between the years 1910 and 1918 as the percentage of positions held by African Americans fell to 4.9 percent. The decline has been attributed in part to practices adopted during the tenure of President Woodrow Wilson (Van Riper 1958). Under President Wilson, the Postal Service and Treasury Department were segregated and federal job applicants were required to submit a photograph with their application. Moreover, President Wilson, like President Taft, declined to appoint African Americans to federal jobs in southern states (Van Riper 1958). Van Riper (1958, 242) found that "there is conclusive evidence that the President, despite public protests and the efforts of many Progressives, fully approved of the segregation measures taken in various departments and agencies." Such overt discriminatory actions offset some of the initial benefits derived from the passage of the merit system.

The first formal policy steps for addressing discriminatory employment practices occurred during the administration of Franklin D. Roosevelt. Under the leadership of A. Philip Randolph, African Americans mobilized to express their dissatisfaction with Department of Defense's employment practices. To avoid the embarrassment of a march on Washington, President Roosevelt passed Executive Order 8802, establishing the Federal Employment Practices Committee to investigate complaints of discrimination (Kellough 1989). A succession of executive orders were passed that slowly expanded the concept of equal employment, culminating in a policy that recommended organizations take positive action to recruit, hire, and promote underrepresented groups (Kellough 1989).[8] Affirmative action programs have been used since the late 1960s to target groups that have been previously excluded or underrepresented. The 1978 Civil Service Reform Act endorsed the notion of representative bureaucracy and further encouraged affirmative action efforts, calling for a " 'a work force reflective of the Nation's diversity' " (Kellough and Rosenbloom 1992, 245).

Since its inception, government has struggled with achieving a more representative bureaucracy and has adopted a variety of policies to reach this goal. The next chapter traces the evolution of the concept of representative bureaucracy in the public administration literature. Particular attention is given to empirical research on the topic.

Notes

1. One notable exception to this view emanates from the theory of congressional dominance (see for example, Barke and Riker 1982; Calvert, McCubbins, and Weingast 1989; Cary 1967; Krause 1996; McCubbins, Noll, and Weingast 1987, 1989; Moe 1987; Ringquist 1995; Weingast and Moran 1983, 1984). Congressional dominance theory is founded upon the premise that agencies are inseparable from legislative committee members and that committee members structure incentives or sanctions, typically in the form of budgetary resources and oversight activities, to elicit agency behavior that conforms to their self-interest (Moe 1987; Weingast and Moran 1983).

2. In this study, bureaucratic power is defined as the influence of administrative agencies in the policy process. The discussion of bureaucratic power is not exhaustive but serves to introduce readers to the complexity and dynamics of the concept, and the dilemma it poses for public administration. Power is a classic concept in political science, public administration, organizational theory, social psychology, as well as other social sciences (see Lukes 1986).

3. For example, overhead democracy (Redford 1969), supremacy of law (Lowi 1969), neutral competence and professionalism (Aberbach and Rockman 1988; Rourke 1992), public choice theory (Ostrom 1973), new public administration (Marini 1971), Blacksburg Manifesto (Wamsley et al. 1990), a constitutional perspective (Cook 1992; Rohr 1986), organizational development (Golembiewski 1969), and public management (Bozeman 1993) have been proposed to legitimate public administration. Each perspective addresses the role of bureaucracy in a democratic society.

4. The discussions of new public administration and public choice are not exhaustive but are aimed to demonstrate different views on administrative responsibility. For a more thorough review of the approaches see, for example, Marini (1971), Waldo (1971), Frederickson (1976), and Ostrom (1973).

5. In a letter to George Frederickson, Frederick Mosher wrote "the term 'new public administration' is presumptuous." The "old" public administration also was concerned with human values, and until at least 1950, leaders were supportive of a government "that [was] representative, responsive, compassionate, [and] concerned with equal opportunity" (Mosher 1992, 200). In Mosher's opinion, the term *new public administration* is a misnomer and he suggests the term *renewed public administration*. In spite of this discord, some important themes evolved from the Minnowbrook conference.

6. By solely focusing on social equity, I acknowledge that I am neglecting other significant themes associated with the new public administration movement. A single agreed-upon model of new public administration, however, does not exist.

7. Gilbert's framework is still relevant for discussing this issue today. This is demonstrated by comparing Meier's (1993b) recent discussion of controlling bureaucratic power with Gilbert's categories of administrative responsibility. Meier (1993b) divided methods of controlling bureaucratic power into two sections: (i) external checks by political institutions, and (2) ethics and participation. Meier's discussion on external checks mirrors Gilbert's formal categories, and his dialogue on ethics and participation is captured in Gilbert's informal categories.

8. For a thorough discussion of the evolution of equal employment opportunity policy, see Kellough (1989).

3

Representative Bureaucracy and the Potential for Reconciling Bureaucracy and Democracy

J. Donald Kingsley's (1944) conception of representative bureaucracy differs significantly from the commonly asserted definition that bureaucracy should be broadly representative of the general public. Since British politics is class based, Kingsley maintained that the bureaucracy should resemble the dominant ruling class in British society. He went so far as to argue that "[n]o group can safely be entrusted with power who do not themselves mirror the dominant forces in society" (1944, 282). To him, the British bureaucracy is representative "when Ministers and Civil Servants share the same backgrounds and hold similar social views" (Kingsley 1944, 273). He reasoned that bureaucrats would be more responsible and responsive to the political desires and platforms of the ministry if they were from similar social classes.

Shortly after Kingsley's work appeared, David Levitan (1946) addressed the issue of achieving a representative public work force in the United States. He contended that recruiting strategies for all positions and branches of the United States government should be "widened and made truly representative of American society" (Levitan 1946, 583). The public, in his opinion, would judge the quality of policies formulated and implemented by a bureaucracy based on its work force composition. Levitan (1946), for example, argued that citizens would receive agencies more favorably if their employees mirrored the composition of society. Agencies, as a result, would experience tangible benefits from having a representative work force.

Norton Long, a prominent scholar in the field of public administration, also addressed the merits of a representative government work force in an essay first published in 1952. He compared the actual representativeness of the bureaucracy to political institutions in the United States. He found that the "bureaucracy may be both more representative of the country and more democratic in composition than the Congress" (Long 1952, 812). Because of this, Long contended that civil servants, as a body, are likely to be more accessible and responsive to the needs and desires of the general public than Congress. It is inevitable, according to Long, that the degree of discretion granted to the bureaucracy will continue to increase. It is therefore vital that the bureaucracy be both representative in composition and in ethos (Long 1952): "By appropriate recruitment, structure, and process the bureaucracy can be made a vital part of a functioning constitutional democracy, filling out the deficiencies of the Congress and the political executives" (Long 1952, 818).

Six years later, Paul Van Riper, in his classic history of the U.S. civil service (1958), also focused on the significance of bureaucratic behavior and attitudes.

> A representative bureaucracy is one in which there is a minimal distinction between the bureaucrats as a group and their administrative behavior and practices on the one hand, and the community or societal membership and its administrative behavior, practices, and expectations on the other. Or to put it another way, the term representative bureaucracy is meant to suggest a body of officials which is broadly representative of the society in which it functions, and which in social ideals is as close as possible to the grass roots of the nation. (Van Riper 1958, 552)

Van Riper failed to fully articulate the underlying linkages between demographic background, attitudes, and behavior, however. Nevertheless, his logic accurately portrayed the basic assumption that when civil servants hold attitudes similar to those of the people whom they represent, their decisions will resemble decisions those they represent would have made under comparable circumstances.

Frederick Mosher (1982), in his work entitled *Democracy and the Public Service*, defined further the concepts raised by Van Riper. Mosher was the first to make explicit the distinction between "passive" representation and "active" representation. Passive representativeness refers to the "origin of individuals and the degree to which, collectively, they mirror the whole society" (Mosher 1982, 12). Mosher (1982) indicated that passive representation was measured easily in terms of education, family income, family social class, race, religion, father's occupation, and similar factors. Representativeness is active when individuals, or civil servants, advocate the interests and the desires of groups sharing their demographic origins. Mosher (1982) acknowledged that he lacked adequate information to determine if an individual's background was linked directly to his or her behavior in the work force. His definition of active representation, however, provided the foundation from which subsequent researchers worked.[1]

In a theoretical exposition of the concept of representative bureaucracy, Kenneth J. Meier (1993c) delineates clearly the potential connection between passive and active representation as outlined in Figure 2.1. As discussed earlier, passive representation (i.e., the demographic composition of the bureaucracy) is important because variations in demographic background are associated with differences in socialization experiences. Individuals' attitudes and values are shaped by their background and socialization experiences. Individuals rely on their values to form decisions, at least in part. Consequently, bureaucrats with different value systems should behave differently.

The literature also suggests a number of other benefits associated with a passively representative bureaucracy. A bureaucracy that reflects the diversity of the general population implies a symbolic commitment to equal access to power (Gallas 1985; Kellough 1990b; Meier 1993c; Mosher 1982; Wise 1990). The symbolic role results from both the personal characteristics of distinctive group members and the assumption that bureaucrats have had experiences in common with other members of that group as a result of these characteristics (Guinier 1994). The use of passive representation as a political symbol makes people believe that the state is just, objective, and democratic. Nesta M. Gallas (1985) even advocates passive representation as a new merit principle of public personnel administration.

Samuel Krislov (1974) argued, however, that examining passive representation is of only limited usefulness; at best, the social origins of civil servants provide only indirect evidence of the representative character of the bureaucracy. Background information reveals little about an adult's abilities or an individual's potential for representing the interests of people with similar backgrounds. A relationship between demographic characteristics and values/attitudes or behaviors of bureaucrats must be established.

Empirical Research on Representative Bureaucracy

Empirical research on representative bureaucracy can be divided into a threefold taxonomy (see Table 3.1). The first collection of studies examines the passive representation of bureaucracies in terms of race, sex, or other demographic factors, and identifies factors that influence the variation of female and minority employment in public organizations. A second group of scholars focuses on the representativeness of policy-relevant attitudes, which serve as a necessary precondition for active representation. Finally, scholars explore the relationship between passive representation and active representation as measured by policy outputs and outcomes.

Research Focusing on Passive Representation

If passive representation refers to the extent to which the bureaucracy reflects the demographic origins of society, a primary question, of course, is which demographic characteristics are most important. In other words, "which characteristics are politically relevant for reproduction" (Pitkin 1967, 87). Kingsley (1944) suggested that socioeconomic class should be the basis for comparing bureaucrats and citizens in England. Krislov (1974) argued, however, that race, ethnicity, and sex were more relevant than class for comparing the composition of the bureaucracy and society in the United States. Overall, the literature has reached a consensus that race and ethnicity are perhaps the most important demographic characteristics for comparing bureaucratic and public representation in the United States (Cayer and Sigelman 1980; Dye and Renick 1981; Herbert 1974; Kranz 1976; Krislov 1974; Meier, 1975, 1993c; Nachmias and Rosenbloom 1973; Rosenbloom and Featherstonhaugh 1977; Rosenbloom and Kinnard 1977; Smith 1980; Thompson 1976, 1978). Lani Guinier (1994, 137) captures the importance of race in this passage:

> Race in this country has defined individual identities, opportunities, frames of reference, and relationships. Where race has been of historical importance and continues to play a significant role, racial-group mem-

Table 3.1

Empirical Research on Representative Bureaucracy

	Examples of Empirical Research in Area	General Findings
Passive Representation:		
Extent to which bureaucracy reflects the demographic composition of society	Subramanian 1967; Hellriegel and Short 1972; Nachmias and Rosenbloom 1973; Gibson and Yeager 1975; Grabosky and Rosenbloom 1975; Meier 1975; Hall and Saltzstein 1977; Rose and Chia 1978; Cayer and Sigelman 1980; Smith 1980; Dometrius 1984; Lewis 1988; Kellough 1990a; Kim 1993; Lewis 1989; Page 1994	Minorities and women are broadly represented in the bureaucracy. However, both minorities and women are underrepresented in upper-level positions.
Determinants of passive representation	Dye and Renick 1981; Eisinger 1982; Welch et al. 1983; Stein 1985, 1986, 1994; Riccucci 1986; Saltzstein 1986; Mladenka 1989a, 1989b, 1991; Kellough 1990a; Kellough and Elliott 1992; Kim 1993; Kim and Mengistu,1994; Cornwell and Kellough 1994; Lewis and Nice 1994	Researchers have explored the impact of various demographic, political, organizational, and economic factors on passive representation. Their findings have been mixed.
Potential for Active Representation:		
Relationship between demographic origins and policy-relevant attitudes	Garham 1975; Meier and Nigro 1976; Rosenbloom and Featherstonhaugh 1977; Rosenbloom and Kinnard 1977; Thompson 1978	Mixed findings: some findings support the relationship between demographic origins and attitudes, while others challenge it.
Active Representation:		
Relationship between passive representation and active representation, as measured by policy outputs and outcomes	Meier and Stewart 1992; Meier 1993a; Hindera 1990, 1993a, 1993b	Presence of minority group significantly related to policy outputs favoring minority group.

bership often serves as a political proxy for shared experience and common interests.

Scholars also maintain that gender is a critical demographic variable in the American bureaucratic setting (Cayer and Sigelman 1980; Daley 1984; Davis and West 1985; Dometrius and Sigelman 1984; Dye and Renick 1981; Hale and Kelly 1989a, 1989b; Kranz 1976; Krislov 1974; Meier 1975, 1993c; Nachmias and Rosenbloom 1980; Rosenbloom and Kinnard 1977; Smith 1980; Thompson 1978). The movement in the 1980s to make public bureaucracies more gender-representative resulted from changing relations between men and women, the changing nature of the economy, and the increased participation of women in the labor force (Duerst-Lahti and Johnson 1992; Duke 1992; Guy 1992; Guy and Duerst-Lahti 1992; Guy and Duke 1992; Hale 1992; Hale and Branch 1992; Hale and Kelly 1989a, 1989b; Johnson and Duerst-Lahti 1992). Thus, examining the passive representation of women in public bureaucracies has become increasingly important (Bayes 1989; Eribes, Cayer, Karnig, and Welch 1989; Hale, Kelly, and Burgess 1989; Hindera 1990; Kawar 1989; Kranz 1976; Stanley 1989).

Researchers have examined a number of other demographic factors, such as age and father's occupation (Daley 1984; Davis and West 1985; Meier 1975; Meier and Nigro 1976; Smith 1980). However, in the American context, race, ethnicity, and to a lesser extent gender are the most salient characteristics because numerous politically relevant attitudes and values are defined along these three dimensions (Meier 1993c).

Since the 1960s, scholars have been studying female and minority representation in U.S. bureaucracies. The first studies focused primarily on race and ethnicity as the demographic characteristics of comparison, but similar approaches were later applied to gauge the representation of women in civil service.

How Does One Measure Passive Representation?

Typically, scholars have employed one of the following methods to compare the racial, ethnic, and gender representativeness of public bureaucracies:

- Percentage female, percentage minority;
- Representative index;

- Measure of variation (MV);
- Lorenz Curve and Gini index of concentration.

Each of these advances a somewhat different way of looking at representation of minorities and women in public organizations. Scholars have used these methods in various contexts to measure minority and female employment in government. As the discussion below illustrates, this body of empirical research informs students of public administration about historic and current trends in minority and female representation in local, state, and federal governments. Although the majority of studies have examined representation generally, some studies have looked at differences in representation by function and organizational level.

Percentage of Minority and Female Civil Servants. A common method used to determine the degree of passive representation is to examine the percentage of bureaucrats who fit into one category of a specific social characteristic (Gibson and Yeager 1975; Hellriegel and Short 1972; Lewis 1988; Nachmias and Rosenbloom 1973; Page 1994; Rose and Chia 1978). Don Hellriegel and Larry Short (1972), for example, looked at the percentage of African-American civil servants and found that African Americans were underrepresented in the federal civil service in both 1940 and 1950, but by 1960 African Americans were slightly overrepresented. African Americans, however, were concentrated in low-level jobs (GS-1–4): in 1960, African Americans held fewer than 1 percent of the jobs at GS-12 or above while they comprised 11.2 percent of the population. Gregory B. Lewis (1988) found that female, African-American, Hispanic, Native American, and Asian federal government employment increased between 1976 and 1986. Furthermore, the share of positions GS-13 and above also grew for each of these groups. The progress of female and minority representation in upper-level positions has been slow, however. Lewis (1988, 705) estimated that "it will take another thirty years at this rate before women and minorities fill half the positions at GS-13 and above." Paul Page (1994) found that in 1991 African Americans staffed 30 percent of GS-1–4 jobs and only 4.5 percent of Senior Executive Service positions (as compared to 12.1 percent of population). Page (1994) remarked that African Americans had made some progress, but that the distribution of African Americans in the federal work force had not changed significantly since 1982.

Representation Index. A second method used to measure passive representation is often referred as the representation index.[2] The ratio is computed as follows:

Representation Index $=$ $\dfrac{\text{\% of a group within the organization}}{\text{\% of a group within the relevant population}}$

A ratio of 1.0 indicates that the composition of the organization corresponds perfectly with the relevant population. The relevant population depends on the study. For example, some studies use national population or local population, while other studies use estimates of the group's share of the appropriate labor pool. V. Subramanian (1967) employed this ratio to gauge the representation of the civil service in Denmark, Great Britain, France, the United States, Turkey, and India. N. Joseph Cayer and Lee Sigelman (1980) also used this approach to determine the representation of African Americans, Hispanics, Asians, and Native Americans in U.S. state and local governments. They found that African Americans and Asians were overrepresented, while Hispanics and Native Americans were underrepresented in 1975. They further examined the representation of these groups by government functions, and learned that minorities were underrepresented in the areas of natural resources, fire, streets and highways, and financial administration and overrepresented in the fields of public welfare, hospitals, housing, corrections, sanitation and sewage, and employment security. Nelson C. Dometrius (1984) continued to focus on bureaucratic representation in state and local governments, but he divided his analysis by organizational grade levels. Overall, according to Dometrius, the representation index improved between 1974 and 1978 for women (.85 to .90), for African Americans (1.08 to 1.28), for Hispanics (.40 to .47), for Asians (1.50 to 2.25), and for Native Americans (.30 to .40). The index for women, African Americans, Hispanics, and Native Americans, however, was much lower when only top-level positions were examined.

Measure of Variation (MV). David Nachmias and David H. Rosenbloom (1973) introduced the "measure of variation" (MV) to assess racial and ethnic integration within public organizations. The measure of variation is estimated by dividing the observed number of racial/ethnic differences in an agency by the "maximum number of differences that could occur given the total number of employees in the agency and equal representation of each racial/ethnic group" (Kellough 1990a, 558). The numerator for the measure of variation is expressed as follows:

$$\Sigma f_i f_j$$

where f is the number of individuals of a certain race or ethnicity, $i, j,$ $k, \ldots$

The denominator is symbolized as follows:

$$\frac{n\,(n-1)}{2} * \left(\frac{f}{n}\right)^2$$

where n is the number of racial or ethnic groups considered, and f is the total number of employees in the agency.

To calculate this measure, one must first determine how many racial and ethnic mixed pairs can be observed in an agency based on the current racial and ethnic composition of the agency's work force. The second step involves dividing this number by the maximum number of differences that could occur if all groups were represented equally in the agency: MV scores can range from 0 to 1. The closer the MV score is to 1, the more equally represented are the groups under investigation.[3] Nachmias and Rosenbloom (1973) found considerable variation in racial and ethnic integration of federal agencies measured by MV. The most integrated agency was the Equal Employment Opportunity Commission, with an MV score of .71. Peter M. Grabosky and David H. Rosenbloom (1975) found that between 1967 and 1973 racial integration of federal agencies improved. The lower grades, however, were more integrated than the upper grades. As Nachmias and Rosenbloom had discovered earlier, the EEOC was the most integrated federal agency in both 1967 and 1973. J. Edward Kellough (1990a) presented similar findings reporting variation in the integration of federal agencies, as well as presenting evidence that the EEOC remained the most integrated federal agency. The EEOC MV score, however, fell slightly between 1973 and 1988, from .76 to .75. The Department of Justice made the most advances in work force integration, improv-

Figure 3.1 Lorenz Curve

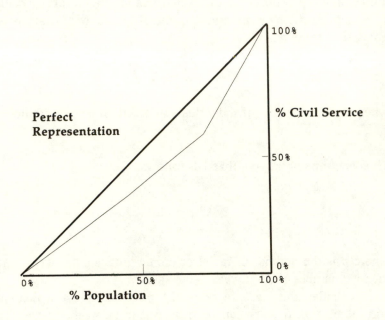

Source: Jennings 1967 in Meier 1975.

ing its MV from .32 to .58, followed closely by the Small Business Administration and the Navy. Pan Suk Kim (1993), also looking at federal agencies, found that Grabosky's and Rosenbloom's (1975) findings were still valid: all minority groups were poorly integrated in the upper tier of the federal work force.

Lorenz Curve and Gini Index of Concentration. Meier (1975) used the Lorenz Curve and Gini index of concentration to explore the degree of representational equality between federal government employment and the general population. The Lorenz Curve presents this information graphically, while the Gini index of concentration provides a numerical summary of the Lorenz Curve. The Lorenz Curve is plotted on two axes, with the horizontal axis representing the percentage of the population having a certain characteristic and the vertical axis representing the percentage of civil servants with the same characteristic. Figure 3.1 displays an example taken from Meier's (1975) research. The 45-degree line indicates perfect representation in terms of father's occupation.[4] The degree to which the Lorenz Curve falls below the 45-degree line illustrates the extent of representational inequality in the organization. In this example, the degree of inequality appears small. Meier concludes (1975, 531) that "the minor deviations from perfect representation are probably the result of minor discriminations or measurement error."

The Gini index of concentration quantifies the information presented by the Lorenz Curve. The Gini index of concentration is the ratio of the area under the 45-degree line and above the Lorenz Curve to the total area of the triangle (Meier 1975; Smith 1980). Scores on the Gini index of concentration range from 0 to 1, with 0 indicating perfect equality of representation (equal to the 45-degree line), and 1 indicating inequality of representation. Meier (1975) concluded that the federal bureaucracy was broadly representative in terms of education, income, age, and father's occupation. However, the degree of equality dropped significantly when examining upper grade levels. Smith (1980) employed this approach to examine representation in state bureaucracies. He found that overall, civil servants in Tennessee, Nebraska, Wisconsin, and Oklahoma were representative of the public in terms of father's occupational status and age, and generally representative in terms of race and sex. When this analysis was limited to upper-level positions, both women and minorities were underrepresented in all of these state bureaucracies.

Although different techniques have been used to measure female and minority representation, the findings have been relatively consistent. Minorities and women are concentrated in lower-level positions and are still vastly underrepresented in top-level decision-making positions within local, state, and federal governments.

Determinants of Passive Representation

In an effort to better understand variation in bureaucratic representation, scholars have devoted substantial effort to discern what factors are related to female and minority employment. In fact, scholars have examined over fifty variables that can be broadly grouped into four categories: demographic, political, organizational, and economic. Most studies have focused on the determinants of minority and female representation in municipal governments, but some studies, though fewer in number, have explored minority and female employment in the federal government.[5] The variables employed in municipal- and federal-level studies sometimes differ because there are a number of factors operating at the municipal level that may not be observable at the federal level given the way federal data are aggregated. For example, municipal governments are geographically contained, and as such, area demographic and political characteristics can be more easily incorporated into the analysis. The following discussion looks at a few factors that have been significantly linked to municipal and federal government employment.

Municipal Government Studies: Minority Group Population. City employment characteristics are influenced by the demographic characteristics of the cities themselves. Thus, the size of the minority population is expected to be a major determinant of the racial composition of the local government work force. In other words, the minority employment share of municipal government jobs will co-vary with the percentage of minorities residing in the city. Overwhelming evidence has been found to support this hypothesis (Dye and Renick 1981; Eisinger 1982; Kim and Mengistu 1994; Lewis 1989; Mladenka 1989a, 1989b, 1991; Riccucci 1986; Stein 1986; Welch, Karnig, and Eribes 1983). Eisinger (1982), for example, produced evidence that the percentage of African Americans in the population was the most important predictor of African-American municipal employment.

Municipal Government Studies: Minority Political Power. Scholars have argued that having minorities in political power will ensure that more and better jobs go to minority residents. Political leaders, according to Lana Stein (1986), often make decisions designed to benefit individuals who have supported them and to ensure future loyalties of constituents. Thus, scholars maintain that increasing minority political representation will lead to greater penetration of minorities in municipal work forces. To test this supposition, scholars have looked at the influence of minorities serving on city councils and the presence of a minority mayor on minority employment. A number of studies found that minority representation on city councils played a significant role in increasing minority employment (Dye and Renick 1981; Mladenka 1989a, 1989b, 1991), and that minority representation on school boards is an important determinant of the presence of minority teachers and administrators (Meier and Stewart 1991; Meier, Stewart, and England 1989). Other studies have demonstrated that the presence of a minority mayor led to more and better jobs for minorities (Eisinger 1982; Lewis 1989; Mladenka 1989a, 1989b; Riccucci 1986). Meier and Smith (1994) challenge the underlying assumption of these studies, contending that a reciprocal relationship exists between political and bureaucratic representation. They argue and find evidence to suggest that minority bureaucratic representation provides "a political base that can be used to elect more minority politicians (bottom-up)" (Meier and Smith 1994, 790 and 801).

Federal Government Studies: Agency Size. In 1975, Grabosky and Rosenbloom reasoned that agency size was inversely related to minority representation because larger agencies would have to hire more minority employees than smaller agencies would to have similar proportional gains in minority representation. Kellough (1990a) found that African-American employment was significantly higher in smaller agencies. Kellough and Elliott (1992) explained that an inverse relationship between agency size and African-American employment may be due in part to the fact that a larger percentage of smaller agencies' work forces are located in Washington, D.C., and agencies located in Washington, D.C., have access to a large pool of qualified African Americans. Their findings support this supposition. Cornwell and Kellough (1994) also found that the percentage of African Americans in the Washington, D.C., labor pool had a positive impact on the growth in African-American employment shares.

Federal Government Studies: Distribution of Occupational Categories. Traditionally, minorities have been overrepresented in blue-collar and clerical jobs, and women have been concentrated in clerical positions. It is expected that the agencies with higher percentages of clerical and blue-collar positions will employ larger shares of women and minorities. Some studies have treated these categories together (Kellough 1990a; Kellough and Elliott 1992), while others have separated the occupational classes (Cornwell and Kellough 1994; Kim and Mengistu 1993). Cornwell and Kellough (1994) showed that federal agencies with larger shares of blue-collar jobs employed more African Americans and Hispanics. When clerical and blue-collar jobs were treated together, Kellough found a positive association between clerical and blue-collar positions and the percentage of African Americans employed in the agency.

An overwhelming amount of the research on representative bureaucracy has focused on passive representation and its determinants (see Table 3.1). Studies at both the municipal and federal levels provide insight into what factors operate to produce differences in minority employment. For example, we know that cities with larger minority populations and more minority elected officials employ more minorities. Due to the nature of political and economic factors available to researchers, studies of municipal employment prove richer in context than federal employment studies. Nevertheless, evidence produced about federal employment contributes significantly to our understanding of minority employment in federal agencies.

Research Focusing on Potential for Active Representation: Values and Attitudes of Civil Servants[6]

While some researchers have focused solely on the demographic composition of the bureaucracy as a test of representation, others have explored attitude congruence between bureaucrats and represented groups. Following the advice of Krislov, Meier, and others, researchers have examined the relationship between demographic characteristics and attitudes.

Kenneth J. Meier and Lloyd Nigro (1976) examined the impact of social background and agency affiliation on attitudes held by bureaucrats. Their research revealed that social characteristics were a poor determinant of attitudes, and that agency affiliation exerted more influence on bureaucrats' attitudes than background characteristics such as race and social class. These results seemed to conflict directly with the theory of representative bureaucracy. There was, however, variation in the findings by policy area and by social characteristics, suggesting that a relationship may exist between policy area and social origins. It is possible that particular traits are more important for shaping attitudes toward certain types of policies, such as race for minority policy issues.

Unlike Meier and Nigro (1976), David Garham (1975) did not specifically test the theory of representative bureaucracy, but he did examine Foreign Service officers' attitudes to determine if they were related to personal background characteristics. He found that region of birth, region of residence, religion, father's occupation, and educational attainment were not related to attitudes. However, this study did not analyze the relationship between attitudes and race or gender. The reason for this exclusion may have been the homogeneous composition of the Foreign Service, and the small number of minorities (n = 3) and women (n = 6) included in the random sample of officers.

David H. Rosenbloom and Jeannette G. Featherstonhaugh (1977) also studied the relationship between demographic characteristics and attitudes. They compared the attitudes of African-American and white bureaucrats and found that significant differences existed. Regardless of organizational position, African-American bureaucrats were more activity oriented. That is, African-American bureaucrats were more likely than their white counterparts to have strong party identification, to try to change local and national laws, to contribute to a political campaign if asked, and to wear a campaign button or display a political bumper sticker. Furthermore, Rosenbloom and Featherstonhaugh examined the attitudes of African-American and white citizens and found that their attitudes differed considerably from the attitudes of civil servants. They did find, however, that when compared to white federal bureaucrats, African-American civil servants tended to hold attitudes similar to African Americans in the general population. Thus, racial background apparently continues to influence the attitudes of individuals after they become civil servants. This research suggests that despite the effects of agency socialization, "social representation can generate active representation of the groups from which the 'passive representatives' come" (Rosenbloom and Featherstonhaugh 1977, 881). Their findings suggest that Meier and Nigro may have been too quick in dismissing representative bureaucracy in all cases.

David H. Rosenbloom and Douglas Kinnard (1977) further investigated this issue by interviewing high-ranking minority Department of Defense (DOD) personnel to determine the extent to which they sought to assist and felt a responsibility toward other minority group members. Seventy-six percent believed that minority members holding high-level positions should attempt to serve the special needs of minorities. The analysis implies that social representation of minorities in upper-level federal positions can be an important means of assuring representation of minorities in society.

Using a sample of public personnel officials from local, state, and federal bureaucracies, Frank J. Thompson (1978) examined civil servants' attitudes toward recruiting and hiring underrepresented minority groups. Social characteristics generally predicted little about an individual's receptivity to hiring minority civil servants. The relation-ships between both sex and race and receptivity of hiring minorities, however, were statistically significant. Nevertheless, because most per-sonal attributes were poor predictors of a civil servant's receptivity to hiring minorities, Thompson (1978) concluded that his findings posed another challenge to the theory of representative bureaucracy.

Research Focusing on Active Representation

Rather than examining the relationship between demographic origins and attitudes as a means of testing the potential for representative bureaucracy, Kenneth Meier and Joseph Stewart (1992) explored the relationship between passive representation and policy outputs and outcomes. Specifically, they examined whether educational bureaucra-cies with different levels of African-American representation produced policies that had differential effects on African-American students. In this research setting, active representation of African Americans, ac-cording to Meier and Stewart, is believed to occur when passive repre-sentation is associated with policy outputs and outcomes benefiting African-American students.

They identified two sets of policy outputs. The first set, ability groupings, included the ratio of African-African students assigned to educable mentally retarded (EMR), trainable mentally retarded (TMR), and gifted classes in school districts. The second set, discipline, in-cluded the ratio of African-American students receiving corporal pun-ishment, in-school suspensions, out-of-school suspensions, expulsions, and referral to courts for prosecution. They also looked at one set of policy outcomes: student performance, which was measured by achievement test scores of third, fifth, eighth, and tenth graders.[7] To assess whether or not African-American teachers and principals en-gaged in active representation, they used multiple regression to control for other factors that also affect ability groupings, discipline, and stu-dent performance. For both ability groupings and discipline, different treatment based on race has been alleged by students and parents, and a number of cases have been litigated (Meier and Stewart 1992). Since these two sets of decisions have been shown to be related to race, educational bureaucracies, according to Meier and Stewart, provide an excellent research setting for examining the linkage between passive and active representation.

The first set of discretionary decisions examined by Meier and Stewart (1992) were ability groupings of African-American students. They hypothesized that school districts with more African-American teachers and principals would enroll fewer African-American students in EMR and TMR classes and more African-American students in gifted classes.

A second policy Meier and Stewart (1992) examined, in which teachers and principals exercise a great deal of discretion, was student discipline. They postulated that as the percentage of African-American principals and teachers increased, the percentage of African-American students disciplined would decrease.

Meier and Stewart (1992) also elected to look at the impact of African-American teachers and principals on student performance. Since prior studies of school districts have shown that African-American students have better access to a quality education in districts with more African-American teachers, Meier and Stewart (1992) hypothesized that achievement test scores of African-American students would be positively associated with the percentage of African-American teachers and principals.[8]

Meier and Stewart (1992) tested the same model for each set of dependent variables. The key independent variables in the analysis were the percentage of teaching faculty that were African American and the percentage of African-American principals in the school system. Because the study included both street-level bureaucrats (teachers) and management-level bureaucrats (principals), Meier and Stewart also tested Thompson's (1976) hypothesis that street-level bureaucrats are more likely to engage in active representation than management-level administrators. Finally, three control variables were introduced into the analysis: percentage of African-American population with a high school diploma, percentage of whites living in poverty, and the ratio of black to white median income. These variables were incorporated because prior research suggested that economic status was related to racial differences in grouping and disciplinary actions (Meier and Stewart 1992).

For EMR and gifted ability groupings, Meier and Stewart (1992) found a significant relationship between passive and active representation at the street level. A higher number of African-American teachers was associated with fewer African-American students in EMR classes and more African Americans in gifted classes.[9] The results for management-level administrators were mixed. The percentage of African-American principals had a negative effect on the number of African-American students assigned to EMR classes, but no relationship was found between representation of African-American principals and placement of African Americans in gifted classes. These findings, according to Meier and Stewart (1992), are consistent with Thompson's supposition that the linkage between passive and active representation is more likely to occur when bureaucrats hold lower-level discretionary jobs.

School districts with more African-American teachers were inclined to impose fewer disciplinary actions against African-American students, a fact that also supports the linkage between passive and active representation. For all five measures of discipline, as the percentage of African-American teachers increased, the number of African-American students disciplined declined. On the other hand, the relationships between African-American principals and the different measures of discipline were unexpected. For out-of-school suspensions, expulsions, and court referrals, there was no relationship. However, both corporal punishment and in-school suspension of African-American students were positively associated with African-American principals. Meier and Stewart (1992, 165) explained:

> Principals and their assistants are responsible for administering discipline in most schools, and administrators who are discipliners receive public praise. . . . This socialization and climate of expectations may well create pressures for black administrators to adopt the norms of the organization enthusiastically and thus be associated with more punishment for black students.

The final set of dependent variables pertained to student performance. The relationships between representation of teachers and principals were consistent across all five achievement tests. African-American teachers were positively associated with higher test scores of African-American students, while the representation of principals had no impact on student performance.

Meier and Stewart's analysis provides considerable evidence that the process of active representation is occurring at the street level of educational bureaucracies. The presence of African-American teachers consistently had a significant influence on policy outcomes and outputs. On the other hand, active representation on the part of management-level bureaucrats (i.e., school principals) was less suggestive. Meier and Stewart (1992) speculated that the divergent findings may be due to the fact that principals may have experienced more organizational socialization.

In a similar study of Latinos, Meier (1993a) expanded his earlier model to address the inconclusive findings regarding the process of active representation of principals. He included an independent variable to test an argument made by Thompson (1976) and Lenneal Henderson (1979) that a critical mass of minority administrators is needed under some circumstances before active representation occurs. According to Meier (1993a), a lack of interaction with and support from other minority administrators may explain, at least in part, the insignificant and negative relationships found earlier.

Meier (1993a) found evidence to support the Thompson/Henderson hypothesis, suggesting that active representation of principals is most likely when a sufficient number of Latino administrators is present in the school district. Meier (1993a) found that the relationship between the presence of minority administrators in an organization and organizational outcomes favoring minority interests is nonlinear. More specifically, Meier found that when only a few minority administrators are present in an organization, policy outputs favoring minority interests decline, but when minority representation becomes larger, and as it continues to increase after that point, policy outputs favoring minority interests increase. Meier suggests that the relationship is negative when only a small number of minority administrators is present because, being only a few, those administrators are less likely to get support from their nonminority co-workers.

He also found a strong linkage between the presence of Latino teachers and the number of Latino students assigned to EMR and gifted classes. Latino teachers had a negative impact on the number of Latino students placed in EMR classes and had a positive effect on the number of Latinos enrolled in gifted courses. Latino principals were also significantly linked to EMR and gifted class assignments, but the direction of the relationship was not as expected. Latino principals were associated with more placement of Latino students in EMR classes and fewer assignments of Latino students to gifted classes.

Meier (1993a) used the same measures of discipline employed by Meier and Stewart (1992), as well as adding an additional measure, alternative education, in this analysis. Overall, the findings were mixed. For in-school suspensions and court referrals, Meier (1993a) found no relationships for Latino teachers, Latino principals, or the Henderson/Thompson hypothesis. On the other hand, the results for the other four types of discipline were consistent with the findings for Latino student assignments to EMR and gifted classes. In all four cases, Latino teachers were negatively related to the discipline ratios, while Latino principals had a significant, positive impact on corporal punishment, out-of-school suspensions, alternative education, and court expulsions. At first, according to Meier, Latino principals were linked with more discipline of Latino students, but as the proportion of Latino principals became larger, fewer disciplinary actions were taken against Latino students (Meier 1993a, 407–408).

The evidence for student performance differed slightly from the findings for ability groupings and discipline of Latino students. These results, however, were consistent with Meier's and Stewart's work on African Americans. As the percentage of Latino teachers in a school district increased, test scores of Latino students improved.[10] For all measures of student performance, the relationship between Latino principals and student performance failed to achieve statistical significance. Moreover, there was no evidence to support the Thompson/Henderson hypothesis for these policy outcomes.

Meier's study (1993a) confirmed that a linkage between passive and active representation is more likely to occur in the lower echelons of an organization. That is, minority bureaucrats exercising discretion in the delivery of goods and services directly to clients are more likely to engage in behaviors that benefit minority clients. This stands in sharp contrast to the evidence presented for management-level minority administrators. Here, the relationship appears more complex. The evidence suggests that a critical mass of Latino administrators is needed to foster active representation at this level.

Using a similar approach, John Hindera (1993a) examined the effect of passive representation of African Americans and women on the distribution of policy outputs in the EEOC. The policy output (dependent variable) investigated was the percentage of total charges filed on behalf of African Americans or women in EEOC district offices. Active representation of a demographic group is believed to occur in the EEOC when passive representation is associated with the percentage of complaints filed on behalf of that group. To control for other factors that might influence the percentage of complaints filed on behalf of a demographic group, Hindera included three control variables in his model: percentage of demographic group within the local employment pool; city size; and ideology of legislators. Hindera hypothesized that the percentage of a demographic group within the local employment pool would have a positive impact on the percentage of complaints filed on behalf of that group. He also postulated that city size would be related to the dependent variable because previous studies have found a relationship between city size and bureaucrats' attitudes toward equal employment opportunity (Hindera 1993a). Hindera, however, did not suggest a directional relationship between city size and EEOC complaints. Finally, he controlled for the political ideology of legislators because "the history of civil rights policy reveals that Title VII has been championed by liberal legislators" (Hindera 1993a, 98).

Hindera (1993a) found that as the employment of African Americans increased, charges filed on behalf of that group also increased. As expected, the percentage of African Americans in the labor pool had a significant, positive effect on the number of complaints filed on behalf of African Americans. Thus, districts serving populations with a larger percentage of African Americans in the labor pool have higher African-American charge levels. City size had a significant, negative impact on EEOC complaints. EEOC districts located in smaller cities filed more charges on behalf of African Africans. The ideology of the House delegate, however, failed to achieve statistical significance in this model. For this policy setting, controlling for other factors that may influence the number of EEOC complaints filed on behalf of African Americans, passive representation of African Americans is linked significantly with policy outputs. Overall, the process of active representation appears to be operating in this environment.

The findings for predicting female active representation were not as hypothesized. The relationship between the percentage of white females in the EEOC and female charge levels was statistically significant, but the direction of the relationship was not as predicted. That is, district offices with more white female investigators filed fewer complaints on behalf of women. Moreover, there was no relationship between black females and the number of complaints filed on behalf of women. Although these findings are suggestive, this is the first study to examine the process of active representation of women. Thus, it is difficult to generalize these findings beyond this case study.

Hindera (1993b) later extended this research to test a slightly different model for African-American and Hispanic representation. As in his previous study, the relationship between passive and active representation of African Americans was significant: as the percentage of African-American investigators increased, the percentage of complaints filed on behalf of African Americans increased. Hindera also added the percentage of white and Hispanic investigators in EEOC district offices to this model: both had a significant, negative impact on the percentage of charges filed on behalf of African Americans. Hindera (1993b, 427) suggested that these findings may be attributed to the fact that a "group might act contrary to another group's interests in a constrained resource environment."

Hindera (1993b) confirmed two other findings from his earlier study. First, city size and the dependent variable were inversely related; that is, EEOC districts located in smaller cities filed more complaints on behalf of African Americans. He also found that the percentage of African Americans in the local labor pool had a significant, positive impact on the number of EEOC complaints filed on behalf of African-American employees.

Hindera (1993b), as mentioned previously, applied this expanded model to explain the percentage of complaints filed on behalf of Hispanics in EEOC district offices. Hispanic employment was positively related to the number of charges filed on behalf of that group, suggesting a linkage between passive and active representation. Unlike his findings for African Americans, there was no relationship between other demographic groups (white and African-American administrators) and Hispanic charge levels. Hindera does not offer a precise explanation for this divergence.

Hindera (1993b) discovered that Hispanic presence in the employment pool influenced allocation patterns of the EEOC, as was the case with African Americans. The results of the Hispanic model, however, differed in that city size did not have a significant effect on the Hispanic charge levels and that there was evidence to suggest that more EEOC complaints were filed on behalf of Hispanics during the Bush administration than during the Reagan administration.

The research of Meier, Stewart, and Hindera strongly suggests that for African Americans and Hispanics, passive representation is linked to active representation at the street level. Meier and Stewart's findings are unclear as to the strength of a comparable relationship for management-level administrators. However, additional examination of the theory of representative bureaucracy at all levels of the organization is needed. Hindera's findings do not offer any support for the process of active representation of women in this research setting, but the relationship should be examined in different organizational contexts and for different policy outputs.

In summary, empirical research designed to test the theory of representative bureaucracy by focusing on demographic origins as predictors of attitudes has yielded contradictory results. This undoubtedly reflects different measures of relevant attitudes. Empirical work examining the impact of passive representation on policy outcomes is more promising, however. The positive relationship found in the literature between street-level minority employment and policy outcomes favoring minority interests supports the basic assumptions of representative bureaucracy. Nevertheless, only a few studies have followed this approach. Findings regarding the relationship between female employment and policy outputs favoring women leave many unanswered questions. Further examination of the theory of representative bureaucracy is warranted to determine whether findings in the current literature can be generalized to other settings.

Notes

1. Since Mosher first discussed the concept of active representation in 1968, at least three other interpretations have been expressed in the literature on representative bureaucracy:
    1. A is considered responsive to B if A acts as B would act if B were in A's position (Meier 1975);
    2. behavior actively represents a community when it increases resources, such as wealth, prestige, or other advantages associated with belonging to that community (Thompson 1976);
    3. active representation occurs when a group of bureaucrats impact policy outputs and outcomes in favor of that group in society (Hindera 1990, 1993a, 1993b; Meier 1993c; Meier and Stewart 1992).

2. Scholars have also referred to this measure as the representative ratio (Sigelman and Karnig 1976), measure of employment parity (Saltzstein 1986; Mladenka 1991), and equal employment opportunity (EEO) index (Lewis 1989).

3. Kellough (1990a, 558) explained, "the strength of the MV lies in the fact that it provides a single figure which shows how close an agency approximates the situation in which there is an equal number of employees from all racial/ethnic groups. The higher the score on the MV, the closer minority representation in

general is to that of nonminority whites and the more racially and ethnically mixed the agency."

4. Meier ordered occupations in ascending order of status: unskilled labor, farm labor, skilled labor, clerical and sales workers, miscellaneous, farm owners, small businessmen, large businessmen, and professionals.

5. A few studies (Dometrius 1984; Smith 1980) have looked at female and minority employment in state bureaucracies, and no research was located that examined minority and female representation in county governments. This is due largely to the difficulty of obtaining comprehensive EEOC data for state and county governments.

6. Other studies have examined attitudinal differences between citizens, private employees, and civil servants (for example, see Garand, Parkhurst, and Seoud 1991; Goodsell 1983; and Lewis 1990), but only studies focusing specifically on representative bureaucracy are reviewed.

7. Meier and Stewart (1992) calculated an equity measure for each dependent variable. The ratio is estimated by dividing the

> probability that a black student will be assigned to a class, subjected to punishment, or perform at a certain level by the probability that any student at random will be so treated or will so perform. This yields the 'odds' that a black student will be in the category under consideration given the overall rate of such categorization in the school system. This ratio is equal to 1.0 when blacks are represented in a category at the same rate as all students in the school system are represented. It is less than 1.0 when they are underrepresented and greater than 1.0 when they are overrepresented. To avoid problems created by extreme values, this odds ratio is subjected to a log transformation. (Meier and Stewart 1992, 162)

8. They explained that the impact of passive representation on student performance may not prove as strong as the impact of African-American representation on ability groupings and discipline because student performance is influenced by a number of factors outside of the school environment.

9. Because of the more "severe" categorization of students for TMR classes, Meier and Stewart (1992) believed that the impact of African-American principals and teachers may be mitigated. The relationship between African-American teachers and TMR ratios was negative, as expected, but failed to achieve statistical significance.

10. Meier used scores for communications and math exams rather than achievement test scores.

4

Representation and the Farmers Home Administration

To conduct a valid empirical test of a theory of representative bureaucracy that poses a connection between demographic backgrounds of administrators and policy outcomes, Meier and Stewart (1992) argue that three conditions must be met. First, the public administrators who are the subjects of the analysis must have a significant amount of discretion in the decision-making process. Second, this discretion must be exercised in an area that has important implications for the group or groups to be represented. As Meier (1993c, 10) explains, a wide variety of socialization experiences are not "relevant to public policy disputes and thus are unlikely to reveal a representational linkage." The third condition necessary for an empirical assessment of the theory is that the administrators be able to be associated directly with the decisions they make. After reviewing the United States Government Manual, a number of programs were identified as possible candidates, and after interviewing program officials from the various programs, the FmHA Rural Housing Loans program was selected as it met the criteria outlined above. Authorized by the Housing Act of 1949, the Rural Housing Loans program provides low-interest loans to moderate- and low-income persons nationwide to buy, build, improve, repair, or rehabilitate rural homes (USDA FmHA, 1993c).

The Farmers Home Administration's (FmHA) mission and goals are "concerned primarily with credit and counseling services . . . building stronger family farms and nonfarm programs to benefit rural families and communities" (USDA FmHA 1990, 1). Charged with protecting the interests of farmers (Meier 1993b), the FmHA is not likely to socialize or instill values in its employees that emphasize representation of minorities and women. However, a number of its programs are directly relevant to minorities and women. The FmHA also has a history of implementing policies that adversely affect African-American farmers (Baldwin 1968; Davidson 1987; Good 1968; Jones 1994; Martin 1985; Myrdal 1969; U.S. Commission on Civil Rights 1965, 1979, 1982). Given the culture and history of the FmHA, this study of the FmHA's Rural Housing Loans program should offer a stringent test of the link between passive and active representation of racial and ethnic minorities and women.

Farmers Home Administration

The FmHA is an agency within the U.S. Department of Agriculture (USDA) that was first responsible for providing loans for farm operating needs and farm ownership (*Agricultural Credit,* 1958). The FmHA's mission was expanded to include rural housing ownership and repair under Title V of the Housing Act of 1949. A congressional finding that "the Federal Housing Administration (FHA) mortgage insurance programs had been ineffective in providing mortgage money to rural and farm areas because of a scarcity of private credit" was influential in the decision to place the programs under the auspices of the FmHA (Jacobs et al. 1986, 14). The Housing Act of 1949 was the first legislation designed specifically to provide residents in rural counties with an opportunity to secure government-backed loans for housing. This law authorized the FmHA to assist families in rural America in acquiring adequate homes (Section 502) and in repairing and improving their existing dwellings (Section 504).

FmHA Rural Housing Loans and Other Programs

The principle underlying the home ownership program, known as Section 502, was to lower the income needed to buy a house by reducing the effective interest rate. To qualify for a 502 loan, the applicant must meet FmHA's definition of very low, low, or moderate income and have been denied credit by a private lender. These income definitions have been adjusted several times over the years. Currently, in a four-person household very low income is defined as not more than 50 percent of a county's median income, while low income is not more

Table 4.1

Rural Housing Loans Program

Year	Funding
1987	$1,052,646,000
1988	1,277,170,000
1989	1,266,863,000
1990	1,411,543,000
1991	2,678,846,000
1992	2,772,440,000
1993	3,092,512,000
1994	3,792,165,000

Source: U.S. Department of Commerce, Bureau of the Census, *Federal Expenditures by State for Fiscal Year 1987, 1988, 1989, 1990, 1991, 1992, 1993, 1994.*

than 80 percent of the county's median income. The moderate-income bracket is estimated by adding $5,500 to the low-income limit.[1] The FmHA also administers repair loans and grants, known as Section 504 assistance. Homeowners may repair, modernize, or improve the safety or sanitation of their homes with a 504 loan. Grants are reserved for persons of very low income over the age of 62, for repairs that remove health and safety hazards.[2]

While FmHA housing loans are available only to residents of "rural" areas, the law has been amended to broaden the manner in which rural areas are defined. Currently, rural areas include any open country or any other town, city, or other place that has fewer than 10,000 residents, even if it is located in a Standard Metropolitan Statistical Area (SMSA). Some towns with populations ranging between 10,000 and 20,000 may qualify if they are located outside of an SMSA and if the area lacks enough mortgage credit for very low-, low-, and moderate-income households. Such a determination is made by the secretaries of the Department of Housing and Urban Development (HUD) and the Department of Agriculture (DOA).

Since its inception, the program has grown to service more communities and a wider range of residents. FmHA has developed a system that today operates through more than 1,700 county offices, over 250 districts, and 46 state offices. Currently, the FmHA distributes more than 50,000 housing loans annually. As illustrated in Table 4.1, the Rural Housing Loans program has been growing steadily since 1987. In 1994, FmHA allocated approximately $3.8 million in housing loans, a 260 percent increase since 1987.

In addition to housing loans and grants, the FmHA administers loans to family farmers, communities, and businesses in rural areas. Some of its farm programs include Farm Operating Loans, Farm Ownership Loans, Soil and Water Loans, and Limited Resources Loans. Rural municipal and county governments, public service districts and authorities, Indian tribal organizations, and community nonprofit organizations are eligible to apply for a series of programs, such as Water and Waste Disposal Loans and Grants, Community Facility Loans, Watershed and Flood Protection Loans, and Resource Conservation and Development Loans. The FmHA also provides development credit to promote economic growth through its Business and Industry Guarantees program. As suggested by the breadth of programs, the FmHA seeks to provide "credit and technical support for rural Americans for improving their farming enterprises, housing conditions, community facilities, and other business endeavors" (USDA FmHA 1990, 1).

Organization of the FmHA and the Rural Housing Loans Program

The FmHA may be more decentralized and "grass roots"–oriented than any other agency in the federal government (Reno 1970). Policy is established at the national level, but more than 1,700 county offices are responsible for interpreting and implementing program directives (Reno 1970; Wyatt and Phillips 1988). Nancy Wyatt and Gerald Phillips (1988), in an insightful case study of organizational communications in the FmHA, found that major responsibilities were divided among the national office, the finance office in St. Louis, and county field offices:

> The national office had to demonstrate to Congress that legislation has been translated into regulations. Often, they had to promulgate policy without really considering its practical consequences. The field offices, on the other hand, had to translate policy into action by dealing face to face with applicants and mortgagees. The finance office had to adhere to federal policy in processing money. Because each unit was preoccupied with its own mission, employees within each component rarely took into account the impact of their actions on other components of the FmHA. Because they existed in separate locations, there was neither opportunity nor necessity to interact on a regular basis with their coun-

terparts in other offices. The national office continued to write ambiguous regulations despite the complaints of the field offices. (Wyatt and Phillips 1988, 83)

The Rural Housing Loans program is administered by county offices representing one or more counties within each state. County offices are grouped administratively into districts, which are then monitored by FmHA state offices. State offices are accountable to the FmHA headquarters located in Washington, D.C.

In October of 1994, President Clinton signed H.R. 4217, the Federal Crop Insurance Reform and Department of Agriculture Reorganization Act of 1994, Public Law No. 103–354. The act authorized the complete reorganization of the Department of Agriculture. As part of this reorganization, the Farmers Home Administration was dissolved and many of its responsibilities, including the Rural Housing Loans program, were transferred to a newly created agency, Rural Housing and Community Service, effective December 1, 1994. FmHA county supervisors' administration of the Rural Housing Loans program did not change when the reorganization took place. However, the Department of Agriculture has consolidated and plans to consolidate more county offices in the future.[3]

FmHA County Supervisors Exercise Discretion and Can Be Linked Directly with Their Decisions

As mentioned previously, the program was selected because it met the three conditions suggested by Meier and Stewart (1992). FmHA county supervisors exert considerable discretion in allocating resources for the Rural Housing Loans program (Hadwiger 1973; Nelson, Lee, and Murray 1973; U.S. Civil Rights Commission 1982; U.S. General Accounting Office 1979; Wyatt and Phillips 1988). They are responsible for reviewing applications, interviewing applicants, and selecting recipients of rural housing loans (USDA FmHA 1993a, 1993b).

The administrative process underlying the housing loan decision is depicted in Figure 4.1. First, after an individual files a loan application with the FmHA, the county office requests a credit report. The county supervisor then interviews the applicant to review his or her case. During the interview, applicants have the opportunity to explain any deficiencies in their credit and/or employment history. Furthermore, the county supervisor assists applicants in completing a budget that

Figure 4.1. **Application Process for FmHA Rural Housing Loans Program**

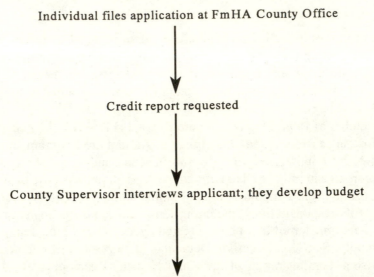

Individual files application at FmHA County Office

Credit report requested

County Supervisor interviews applicant; they develop budget

County Supervisor determines whether the applicant is eligible for a loan

will demonstrate their repayment abilities. The county supervisor then renders a decision as to whether an applicant is eligible for a rural housing loan given his or her income level, credit history, employment, and repayment ability.

Obviously, some decisions regarding eligibility are apparent. Individuals with incomes exceeding the low to moderate levels targeted by the program or applicants without adequate repayment ability will be classified as ineligible. Similarly, individuals falling within the low- to moderate-income level who have a good credit history and the ability to make house payments will be classified as eligible. Applicants with a poor credit history and/or irregular employment could often be ruled in either direction, however. These cases require the county supervisor to make a decision based on his or her personal judgment of the situation.[4] A number of subjective factors can enter into the decision. For example, Wyatt and Phillips (1988, 92) found that "one county supervisor . . . would regularly deny loans to families she saw eating at fast-food restaurants. 'Eating out,' she told us, 'is not good money management, and it is bad nutrition.'" When making such decisions, county supervisors receive no direct oversight from district office staff and minimum attention from state office personnel.

Survey results confirm that county supervisors are granted discretion in implementing the Rural Housing Loans programs. Ninety-four percent of southern FmHA county supervisors surveyed indicated that they had considerable discretion in allocating resources for the Rural Housing Loans program. Final loan determinations are the sole responsibility of county supervisors; therefore, these decisions can be linked directly with an individual bureaucrat, providing an ideal situation in which to examine the theory of representative bureaucracy.

Discretion Exercised in Salient Policy Area for Minorities and Women

The Rural Housing Loans program provides tangible benefits to those who receive the loans. Since housing absorbs a larger percentage of lower-income individuals' budgets than of individuals with higher incomes, these benefits are particularly significant to this target population, which has fewer opportunities for other investments (Jackson and Jackson 1986). Home ownership is a primary method of capital investment for people of low income (Jackson and Jackson 1986) because financial benefits accrue from housing equity and from the tax savings of owning a home. Scholars also purport that home ownership leads to sociopsychological benefits, which are derived from the "role that housing plays in communicating, if not defining, social status in the American society" (Rohe and Stegman 1994, 153). Individuals who own their own homes are thought to have higher social standing, which subsequently leads to higher self-esteem and satisfaction (Rohe and Stegman 1994). Given both the tangible and intangible benefits associated with homeownership, it important to briefly consider historical patterns of housing quality and access in the United States.

There are significant differences in the type and quality of housing generally occupied by African Americans and Caucasians: Suzanne Bianchi, Reynolds Farley, and Daphne Spain (1986, 19) explained that "blacks typically live in lower quality housing than whites, occupy older housing, and are less likely to own their own homes." Historically, it has been more difficult for certain minority and ethnic groups to acquire housing than for Caucasian citizens.[5] Patterns of racial and ethnic segregation in residential housing markets and discrimination against minority groups by mortgage lenders have been a longstanding civil rights concern (Hula 1991; Momeni 1986; Squires 1992, 1994). Both Title VIII of the Civil Rights Act of 1968 and the Equal Credit Opportunity Act of 1976 clearly prohibit discrimination against mortgage loan applicants on the basis of race or nationality.

Nevertheless, numerous cases of alleged discrimination have been documented. For example, the *Los Angeles Times* examined Federal Reserve Board records for nearly 200,000 applications for mortgages, home improvement, and refinancing loans in Los Angeles County processed in 1990 (Rosenblatt, Morris, and Bates 1992) and found that African Americans were rejected for home mortgage loans more often than members of other ethnic groups at every income level. Overall, Asian Americans and Caucasians have the highest acceptance rates for housing loans (Rosenblatt, Morris, and Bates 1992).

Richard Schroeder (1993) reported that 22 percent of African-American applicants for mortgages were rejected in Erie County, New York, compared to an 8 percent rejection rate for Caucasians in 1992. Schroeder (1993) detailed efforts on the part of several private lenders to combat the disparity in rejection rates between minority and nonminority groups. KeyCorp Mortgage Inc., for example, made an effort to employ more minority mortgage underwriters in order to avoid unintentional bias in lending decisions. Similarly, Gay Greene, senior vice president with Sibley Mortgage Corp., explained that "'we have to sensitize staffs of lenders to ensure the elimination of unintentional bias'" (Schroeder 1993, 12). But despite efforts by private lending firms and the federal government, disparities in rejection rates between racial and ethnic groups persist (Schroeder 1993; Gugliotta 1994).

A recent study of 1992 Home Mortgage Disclosure Act (HMDA) data revealed that the rates of denial for home ownership and improvement loans varied among racial and ethnic groups.[6] Glenn Canner, Wayne Passmore, and Dolores Smith (1994) found that white applicants in all income groups had lower rates of denial than African-American or Hispanic applicants. As Canner, Passmore, and Smith (1994, 80) noted, "these disparities raise the possibility of unlawful discrimination against some minority applicants." Their analysis also showed that, among racial and ethnic groups, African Americans were most likely to seek government-backed home ownership loans. Of all African-American applicants, 41 percent applied for government-backed loans, compared to 31 percent of Hispanics, 23 percent of Native Americans/Alaskan Natives, 21 percent of whites, and 11 percent of Asians/Pacific Islanders. Canner, Passmore, and Smith (1994, 84) suggested that "one possible explanation for this relatively greater reliance of black applicants on government-backed programs is that black households, on average, have smaller holdings of liquid assets compared with those of other low-income households." The data also suggest that minorities may pursue government-backed loan programs because these programs have lower denial rates than private lending sources.[7] For example, 24 percent of African-American, 19 percent of Hispanic, 18 percent of Native American/Alaskan Native, 14 percent of Asian/Pacific Islander, and 13 percent of white applicants were denied government-backed loans, whereas 36 percent of African-American, 27 percent of Hispanic, 27 percent of Native American/Alaskan Native, 15 percent of Asian/Pacific Islander, and 16 percent of white applicants were denied mortgage loans by nongovernmental lending sources. Despite the fact that government-sponsored programs had lower denial rates for all groups, these programs still had higher denial rates of racial and ethnic minority applicants than of white applicants.

Several studies have documented specific findings of discrimination in the FmHA in terms of the services provided to African Americans compared to those provided to similarly situated Caucasians (Baldwin 1968; Good 1968; Myrdal 1969; U.S. Commission on Civil Rights 1965, 1979, 1982). For example, Sidney Baldwin (1968) discovered disparate patterns of lending in the Farm Security Administration, which was dissolved in 1946 and its responsibilities and personnel transferred to the then newly created Farmers Home Administration (U.S. Commission on Civil Rights 1982). He found that "a white low-income farm family had a two-to-one advantage over a Negro family in obtaining a standard loan. The odds against a Negro family ranged from three-to-one in Tennessee to seven-to-one in Mississippi" (Baldwin 1968, 201). More recently, African-American farmers in North Carolina alleged that they suffered "from a range of discriminatory actions, and [were] subjected to disrespect, embarrassment, and humiliation by FmHA officials" (U.S. Commission on Civil Rights 1982, 84).

In the mid-1950s, African-American veterans' groups protested that local FmHA offices were discriminating against African-American borrowers. The agency responded by placing African-American professionals in several southern states to serve as "'supervisors-at-large' to initiate loan applications for blacks in offices where local supervisors were unwilling to do so" (Hadwiger 1973, 51). In a 1973 study of African-American FmHA county supervisors, Don F. Hadwiger (1973, 53) found that African-American supervisors believed that their presence had a favorable impact on black participation. They explained that blacks had previously been afraid to approach some all-white offices. These findings suggest that employing minority county supervisors may improve lending patterns to minority clients.

A 1982 study by the U.S. Commission on Civil Rights found that the Department of Agriculture and, specifically, the FmHA had "failed to integrate civil rights goals into program objectives" (U.S. Commission on Civil Rights 1982, iv). The report noted that the FmHA had "a reputation for discriminatory lending" (U.S. Commission on Civil Rights 1982, 63). An earlier report by the commission was also critical of the FmHA's limited distribution of housing loans to African Americans and suggested that FmHA staff training and minority outreach programs were unsatisfactory (U.S. Commission on Civil Rights 1979).

The recent literature on discrimination in the mortgage lending industry has concentrated on racial and ethnic minorities and has devoted less attention to the treatment of women. Housing is an important issue for women as they have had trouble historically gaining credit approval from lending institutions (Ahrentzen 1985; Birch 1985, 1989; Conway, Ahern, and Steuernagel 1995; Gelb and Palley 1982; Shalala and McGeorge 1981; Stegman 1985; Weiss 1980). In addition to credit discrimination, Sherry Ahrentzen (1985) found that women were significantly more likely than men to encounter discrimination when searching for a place to live. Furthermore, Ahrentzen (1985, 72) contended that the needs of "these housing consumers differ from those of the traditional two-parent household and that these needs are neglected in a market attuned to the status quo." Female-headed households typically have fewer economic and social resources than traditional two-parent households (Ahrentzen 1985; Weiss 1980). Between 1980 and 1993, the percentage of single mothers living below the poverty line climbed 32 percent (U.S. Department of Commerce 1994). Similarly, the percentage of female-headed households increased by 37 percent between 1980 and 1993 (U.S. Department of Commerce 1994).

Employment Opportunities in the FmHA

Since the FmHA is not normally thought of as an agency with a mission emphasizing minority and female representation, despite the direct

Figure 4.2. **Representation of African Americans**

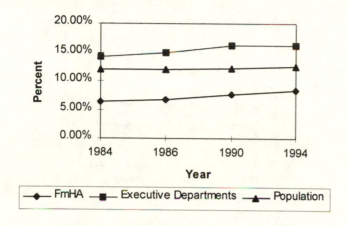

relevance of its programs to minorities and women, it offers a rigorous test of the viability of the theory of representative bureaucracy. In fact, the history and organizational context of the FmHA suggest that the representation of minority interests may be suppressed at the agency. The Department of Agriculture itself is one of the more poorly integrated organizations within the federal government and has been among the slowest to expand employment opportunities for minorities and women (Kellough 1990a, 1990b). When examining employment patterns of the FmHA, an agency within the USDA, a similar pattern emerges. Figures 4.2 to 4.6 illustrate the percentages of African Americans, Hispanics, Asian Americans, Native Americans, and women working for the FmHA, occupying positions in federal executive departments, and comprising the general population. African Americans, Asian Americans, Hispanics, and women have been proportionately underrepresented in the FmHA; that is, the percentage of the group employed by the FmHA is less than the percentage of the group within the population in 1984, 1986, 1990, and 1994. Compared to other federal agencies, proportionately fewer African Americans, Asian Americans, Hispanics, and Native Americans have been employed by the FmHA. Relative to other federal agencies, however, women have fared better in securing jobs in the FmHA. Native Americans were the only minority group that was overrepresented in the FmHA; that is, the percentage of Native Americans employed by the

Figure 4.3. **Representation of Hispanics**

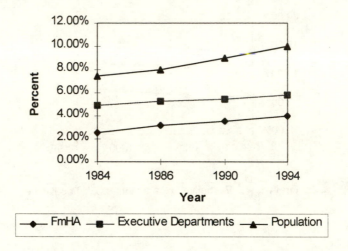

Figure 4.4. **Representation of Asian Americans**

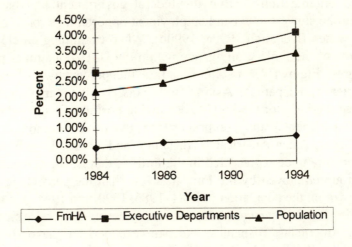

Figure 4.5. **Representation of Native Americans**

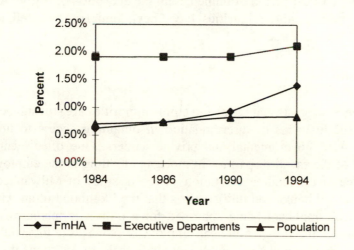

Figure 4.6. **Representation of Women**

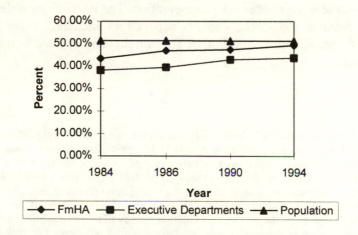

FmHA exceeded the percentage of the group within the population. For the ten-year period examined, with the exception of Native Americans, women and minorities have been underrepresented in the FmHA's work force.

Conclusions

Evidence suggests that racial and ethnic minorities are still subject to at least subtle forms of discrimination in obtaining access to housing loans from governmental and private lenders. One often-mentioned cause of the racial disparities in mortgage lending is the employment practice of the lending institution. A recent study of Milwaukee area commercial banks and thrifts shows that the likelihood of an African-American applicant being approved for a mortgage increases as the proportion of African-American employees increases in financial institutions (Squires and Kim 1995). This study seeks to determine if FmHA districts with larger shares of minority decision makers award more loan eligibility determinations to minorities. The analysis in this study is divided into two parts. Chapter 5 focuses on passive representation of minorities and women in FmHA districts and its relationship to active representation. Chapter 6 moves beyond previous research to explore the process of active representation. The research considers the role demands and conflicts county supervisors encounter when trying to both participate in the FmHA's hierarchy and represent minority interests.

Notes

1. The houses typically financed by the FmHA are modest in size, design, and cost, and the loans generally have a term of 33 years for repayment. Loan terms, however, may be extended up to a maximum of 38 years for applicants whose adjusted annual income does not exceed 60 percent of the area's median income and who need the extra time to repay to the loan. Loans do not necessarily require a down payment, and the FmHA can lend up to 100 percent of the market property value of the home. Interest credit is also available to qualified very low- and low-income borrowers in order to make housing payments fall within their range of repayment ability.

2. Section 504 loans cannot exceed $15,000, and the loan terms cannot be greater than twenty years.

3. This study will continue to refer to the organization as the FmHA to avoid confusion.

4. The United States General Accounting Office (1993) recently reported that there were variations in the implementation of the FmHA Rural Housing Loan programs among local offices because of the extent of subjectivity exercised by local supervisors in making decisions.

5. For example, until 1950, the Code of Ethics for Realtors prohibited real estate agents from "being instrumental in introducing into a neighborhood . . . members of any race, nationality, or any individual whose presence will clearly be detrimental to property values in that neighborhood" (Brown 1992, 1).

6. Among the 9,073 lending institutions that submitted information, 5,468 were commercial banks, 1,395 savings associations, 1,706 credit unions, and 504 mortgage companies.

7. Government programs include loans backed by the Federal Housing Administration, the Department of Veterans Affairs, and the Farmers Home Administration.

5

Testing the Linkage Between Passive and Active Representation

Implicit in the study of passive representation is the notion that it leads to more active forms of representation (Meier, Stewart, and England 1989). However, having a passively representative agency does not necessarily guarantee that it will make decisions reflecting the interests of those represented. To determine conditions under which passive representation is linked to active representation, scholars have began to explore empirically the correspondence between agency employment characteristics and agency outputs. This chapter builds upon these earlier efforts by examining the linkage between passive and active representation in the Farmers Home Administration. The unit of analysis is districts, of which there are 246 included in the analysis.[1] Districts are comprised of a number of county offices.

The analysis will concentrate on the following questions. First, to what extent are Caucasians, African Americans, Hispanics, Asian Americans, Native Americans, and women represented in overall FmHA district employment, in FmHA county supervisor positions, and in FmHA lower-level district positions? Second, what factors account for the variation in representation of African Americans, Hispanics, Asian Americans, Native Americans, and women in FmHA district employment? Third, how does the passive representation of a particular group affect the distribution of policy outputs to that group? For example, are a higher percentage of Hispanics deemed eligible to receive rural housing loans in districts employing a larger percentage of Hispanic county supervisors?

Passive Representation in FmHA Districts

Previous studies of minority and gender employment patterns guide this present endeavor (see Chapter 3 for a more detailed discussion of this body of research). The discussion of passive representation is limited to measuring the degree to which racial and ethnic minorities and women are represented in FmHA district employment, including as county supervisors as well as in lower-level positions in FmHA offices, such as assistant county supervisors, technicians, office assistants, and office automation clerks.[2] Variation in the representation of African Americans, Hispanics, Asians, Native Americans, and women does exist between districts. For example, the percentage of African-American county supervisors working in FmHA districts ranges from 0 to 63, and the percentage of Hispanic county supervisors employed in districts varies from 0 to 100 (see Table 5.1 for the mean and standard deviation of the percentage of each group employed by category).

The most common method of examining the racial, ethnic, and gender representativeness of public bureaucracies is the representation index (see Chapter 3). The representation index is calculated by dividing the percentage of a particular group within the organization by the percentage of that group within the relevant population. A ratio of 1.0 suggests that the representation of a group within an organization corresponds exactly with its representation in the relevant population. An index of less than 1.0 indicates underrepresentation of a group, while a ratio of more than 1.0 indicates overrepresentation of a group.

Table 5.2 presents the nationwide representation indexes for Caucasians, African Americans, Hispanics, Asian Americans, Native Americans, and women in overall FmHA district employment, in county supervisor positions, and in lower-level positions. The representation index for Caucasians, Native Americans, and women exceeds 1.0, indicating that these groups are slightly overrepresented in both FmHA district employment and lower-level positions. Only white and Native American citizens are overrepresented as county supervisors. African Americans, Asian Americans, Native Americans, and women are better represented in lower-level positions. This finding is consistent with previous research on work force representation in local, state, and federal government. Of the groups underrepresented as county supervisors, the largest disparities in representation between the key decision-making position of county

Table 5.1

Means and Standard Deviations of Percentage of Groups Employed

	Mean	Standard Deviation	Percentage of Offices Without
District Employees			
White	87.8	13.6	00.0
African-American	6.1	9.1	45.9
Hispanic	3.4	10.0	71.1
Asian-American	0.7	5.2	87.8
Native American	1.9	3.9	65.4
Women	72.8	6.4	00.0
County Supervisors			
White	90.5	16.9	00.0
African-American	8.4	15.0	69.1
Hispanic	3.7	13.6	88.2
Asian-American	0.7	4.9	97.2
Native American	1.0	5.0	95.1
Women	14.2	15.5	41.6
Lower-Level Positions			
White	87.1	14.3	00.0
African-American	6.3	9.6	47.8
Hispanic	3.6	10.5	73.9
Asian-American	0.8	5.6	88.2
Native American	2.2	4.5	67.8
Women	74.4	7.2	00.0

supervisor and lower-level, non-decision-making positions exist for women, Asian Americans, and African Americans.

Identifying Variables Possibly Associated with Passive Representation

Although numerous studies have examined the employment of minorities and women in local, state, and federal agencies, little attention has been paid to employment variation within a federal agency (Cornwell and Kellough 1994; Kellough 1990a; Kellough and Elliott 1992). This study seeks to fill this gap by examining the representation of minorities and women across FmHA district offices, with a model based on previous research. As illustrated in Figure 5.1, the model suggests that work force representation is a function of four sets of variables: demographic, economic, organizational, and political.

Table 5.2

Passive Representation of Racial, Ethnic, and Gender Groups among FmHA District Employees, County Supervisors, and Lower-Level District Employees

Representation Index	Caucasians	African Americans	Hispanics	Asians	Native Americans	Women
Districts	1.0855	.5633	.3334	.2207	2.1519	1.2900
County Supervisors	1.0765	.4792	.3370	.0886	1.0875	.2617
Lower-level District Positions	1.0884	.5746	.3333	.2474	2.3801	1.519

Note: The representation index for each group was calculated by dividing the percentage of FmHA employees in a group by the percentage of the national population comprised of that group.

Figure 5.1. **A Model of Work Force Representation**

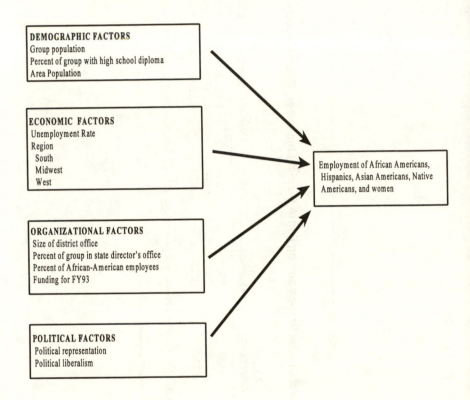

DEMOGRAPHIC FACTORS
Group population
Percent of group with high school diploma
Area Population

ECONOMIC FACTORS
Unemployment Rate
Region
South
Midwest
West

ORGANIZATIONAL FACTORS
Size of district office
Percent of group in state director's office
Percent of African-American employees
Funding for FY93

POLITICAL FACTORS
Political representation
Political liberalism

Employment of African Americans, Hispanics, Asian Americans, Native Americans, and women

Demographic Factors

Minority or Gender Group Population. The size of the minority or gender group population has been noted as a significant factor in increasing minority and gender employment (Dye and Renick 1981; Eisinger 1982; Kim and Mengistu 1994; Lewis 1989; Meier and Stewart 1991; Meier, Stewart, and England 1989; Mladenka 1989a, 1989b, 1991; Riccucci 1986; Stein 1986; Welch, Karnig, and Eribes 1983). Most scholars have argued that a group's work force representation is dependent on the size of the group's population in the area. In other words, agency offices located in areas with larger populations of minorities and women are likely to employ more minorities and women. For example, merely having a larger proportion of Native Americans residing in a district should increase the probability of receiving more job applications from Native Americans and, subsequently, hiring more Native Americans. As a result, the number of jobs held by Native Americans in these areas is likely to exceed the number of positions occupied by Native Americans in areas with fewer Native American residents. Overwhelming evidence has been found to support this hypothesis in municipal research (Dye and Renick 1981; Eisinger 1982; Kim and Mengistu 1994; Lewis 1989; Mladenka 1989a, 1989b, 1991; Riccucci 1986; Stein 1986; Welch, Karnig, and Eribes 1983). More recently, Meier, Stewart, and England (1989) have made a different, but equally compelling, argument to support the importance of size of a minority's local population. Representation in policy-making positions is depicted, in part, as a function of a group's political resources as measured by a group's size or educational level (Meier and Stewart 1991; Meier, Stewart, and England 1989). A group is likely to have more political clout in areas where its population is higher and, therefore, is better able to use its influence to secure a larger share of government jobs (Meier, Stewart, and England 1989). For the reasons outlined, the impact of the proportion of minorities and women residing in a district is considered in subsequent analyses of minority and female employment.

Percentage of Racial or Ethnic Minority Group with a High School Diploma. The ability of minority groups to compete for and secure jobs is affected by their educational attainment (Lewis and Nice 1994; Meier 1975). Offices located in districts with a better-educated minority labor pool have more qualified minority applicants to select from and, therefore, are more likely to employ a larger share of minority group members. Several scholars have also argued that educational attainment is an indicator of political resources because increased education has been linked to greater voter participation (Meier and Stewart 1991; Meier, Stewart, and England 1989). Studies examining the relationship between minority employment and education level have produced conflicting results (Dye and Renick 1981; Eisinger 1982; Hall and Saltzstein 1977; Lewis and Nice 1994; Meier 1975; Meier and Stewart 1991; Meier, Stewart, and England 1989; Mladenka 1989a). Peter Eisinger (1982) found that, in the case of professional and administrative positions in municipal governments, educational characteristics of the African-American population had no independent effect on African-American employment. However, Gregory Lewis and David Nice's (1994) research indicated the opposite. Their research suggests that as the percentage of high school graduates of a particular group increases, the segregation index of that group decreases. One factor that may explain the difference in findings may be related to other job opportunities. Not only will more educated minorities be more competitive for public sector positions, they will be more competitive for jobs in the private sector. However, since FmHA districts serve rural areas that tend to attract less commercial and industrial development and because federal government jobs are stable and relatively well paid, group employment is expected to be a function of a group's educational level.

Total Population. In studies of municipal employment, scholars have suggested that city size is an important predictor of minority and gender work force composition (Dye and Renick 1981; Eisinger 1982; Kim and Mengistu 1994; Mlandenka 1989a, 1989b, 1991; Stein 1985). Larger areas should have larger government work forces and more turnover, which makes them more likely to employ more minorities and women (Stein 1985). However, most research has not shown a statistically significant relationship between area population and employment patterns. Although previous findings are lackluster, the relationship is reexamined in this study.

Economic Factors

Unemployment rates. Research has also identified unemployment rates as a significant economic variable in studies of minority and gender work force representation (Kim and Mengistu 1994; Stein 1985). Pan Suk Kim and Berhanu Mengistu (1994, 166) argue that the average unemployment rate "is a reasonable indicator of fiscal constraints." Stein (1985) contends that areas with higher unemployment rates would be less able to hire minorities and, therefore, would employ fewer minorities. Contrary to expectation, however, Stein (1985) did not find a relationship between unemployment rate and minority representation. Similar research published nine years later yielded analogous results (Kim and Mengistu 1994). The employment characteristics of the area did not affect the percentage of African Americans, Hispanics, and Asian Americans working in law enforcement agencies (Kim and

Mengistu 1994). However, this same study reported evidence that women captured a greater share of law enforcement positions in areas with higher unemployment rates (Kim and Mengistu 1994). Because previous research has yielded inconsistent results, the effect of area unemployment rates on passive representation will be investigated here.

Region. It is also likely that region will be linked to minority and gender work force representation. Stein (1985) suggests that economies in the south and west, or the sunbelt region, have been prospering, while the economic conditions in the northeast and midwest, or the rustbelt region, have lagged behind. Several scholars, however, have noted that the effects of the growing economy in the south may be mitigated in part by a history of discriminatory employment practices (Sigelman and Karnig 1976; Riccucci 1986). A number of studies have examined the relevance of region to local and state work force composition, and the empirical findings have been mixed (Kim and Mengistu 1994; Lewis 1989; Riccucci 1986; Saltzstein 1986; Stein 1985; Warner, Steel, and Lovrich 1989). Norma Riccucci (1986) found that women and minorities were significantly less represented in city police forces in the south, whereas Warner, Steel, and Lovrich (1989) discovered higher percentages of female officers employed in cities located in the southern and central regions of the country. More recently, Kim and Mengistu (1994) found that female and Hispanic employment in law enforcement agencies was lower in northeastern cities, while African-American employment was higher in southern cities. In terms of federal employment practices, recent research has included two regional measures—share of agency positions located in the southwest and in Washington, D.C. These variables, however, were included as proxy indicators of the relevant labor market rather than as economic indicators (Cornwell and Kellough 1994; Kellough and Elliott 1992). Although scholars have not explicitly examined regional differences in federal employment patterns, representation of all minority groups and women is expected to be higher in the south and west than in the northeast because of the loss of jobs and job opportunities associated with the decline of industrial investments.

Organizational Factors

Organizational Size. In 1975, Grabosky and Rosenbloom reasoned that agency size was inversely related to minority representation because larger agencies would have to hire more minority employees than smaller agencies in order to have similar proportional gains in minority representation. Kellough (1990a), for instance, found that African-American employment was significantly higher in smaller agencies. In a similar study, Kellough and Elliott (1992) concluded that the inverse relationship between agency size and African-American employment was an artifact since a larger percentage of smaller agencies' work forces are located in Washington, D.C. Since agencies located in Washington, D.C., have access to a large pool of qualified African Americans, smaller agencies are likely to employ more African Americans. Contrary to earlier research by Kellough (1990a) and Kellough and Elliott (1992), Kim (1993) found that agency size was statistically unimportant in explaining African-American, Hispanic, and female employment, but was a positive and significant determinant of Asian-American employment in federal agencies. It is plausible that larger agencies may be hiring more personnel in an absolute sense, and, since Asian Americans, on average, are better educated than other minority groups, they may comprise a larger share of the pool of qualified applicants (Hraba 1994). Since this study focuses on the work force composition of district offices within one agency, and for the reasons raised by Grabosky and Rosenbloom (1975), the share of positions held by minorities and women is expected to be inversely related to organizational size.

Presence of Minorities and Women in State Director's Office. Several studies have suggested that minorities sense a need or feel a responsibility to promote practices that increase minority group representation (Martinez 1991; Murray et al. 1994). Sylvester Murray et al. (1994), for instance, found that all but one of 160 individuals responding to their survey reported that they recommend or advocate policies that address the needs of minorities. Minority or female leaders at the state level may be more sensitive to the needs and interests of minorities and women and, as a result, adopt personnel policies and practices that promote minority and gender work force representation. Several studies have shown that administrators tend to hire individuals from similar backgrounds (Dye and Renick 1981; Meier, Stewart, and England 1989; Saltzstein 1983; Thompson 1978). Meier, Stewart, and England (1989) found that school districts with more African-American school administrators employed more African-American teachers. However, in a recent study of federal agencies, Kim (1993) did not discover a relationship between Senior Executive Service (SES) representation and agency representation of Hispanics, African Americans, and women. Moreover, this research revealed that as the percentage of SES positions held by Asian Americans increased, the percentage of Asian Americans in the agency work force declined significantly.

Competitive Minority Group. Scholars have also examined the extent to which African Americans and other minority groups compete for scarce resources, such as jobs (Kim 1993; McClain 1993; McClain and Karnig 1990; Mladenka 1989a, 1989b; Rosenbloom 1973; Welch et al. 1983). The empirical research on work force integration suggests that in some cases, African Americans and other ethnic groups compete for jobs and in other cases, they do not. For example, Susan Welch, Albert Karnig, and Richard Eribes (1983) found that Hispanic employment was higher in cities with smaller shares of municipal jobs held by African-American males, whereas Kim's (1993) research revealed that the percentage of black employment was not significantly linked to employment of Asian Americans and Hispanics in federal agencies. This study will explore whether or not districts that employ a larger number of African Americans have fewer Hispanic, Asian-American, Native American, and female personnel.

Funding. Districts that receive more funding are likely to have more resources for hiring new personnel as well as slack resources that could be used to provide training and other opportunities for personnel development. Since previous research indicates that minorities and women are typically concentrated in lower-level positions, funding may enable units to administer training curriculums that help employees advance or progress within the agency. In a study of state segregation levels by race and gender, Lewis and Nice (1994) tested a similar hypothesis and found that slack resources, as measured by state median income, were not significantly related to segregation indexes of the nine groups examined. This research will examine the relationship between district funding and passive representation.

Political Factors

Political Representation. It has been argued that having minorities in political power will ensure that more and better job opportunities are provided to minority residents. Scholars have looked at the influence of minorities serving on city councils and the presence of a minority mayor on minority employment. A number of studies found that minority representation on city councils played a significant role in increasing minority employment (Dye and Renick 1981; Mladenka 1989a, 1989b, 1991), and others have demonstrated that the presence of a minority mayor led to more and better jobs for minorities (Eisinger 1982; Lewis 1989; Mladenka 1989a, 1989b; Riccucci 1986). To date, the relationship between political representation and bureaucratic representation in federal agencies has not been examined. This study posits that minorities and women will hold a larger share of positions in districts represented by a minority or woman in the U.S. House of Representatives.

Political Ideology. Political ideology may also be an important determinant of minority and gender employment. Lewis and Nice (1994, 398) contend that "in general, liberals emphasize equality and support government efforts to promote it more than do conservatives. Conservatives tend to be more skeptical about both equality and the relative costs and benefits of policies designed to foster it." A 1994 study revealed that political conservatism of a state was associated with higher segregation of African-American males, African-American females, and Hispanic males (Lewis and Nice 1994). As evidenced in the current debates on affirmative action, liberal members of Congress are fundamentally predisposed toward support for policies promoting the employment of minorities and women, while conservative members are less inclined to support such practices.[3] Given that FmHA state and district employees are sensitive to the political positions of elected officials representing their jurisdictions, minorities and women should occupy a greater share of positions in districts represented by more liberal members of Congress. The present study uses the 1993 Americans for Democratic Action (ADA) rating of each FmHA district's House of Representatives member as a measure of liberalism. The index is scaled from 0 (conservative) to 100 (liberal). For districts in which more than one delegate represents the area, a weighted ideology index is constructed based on the proportion of the population of the district that each delegate represents.[4]

Summary

Group employment is therefore modeled as a function of group population size, group education, area population size, unemployment rate, region, size of district office, state office work force representative, interminority competition, funding, political representation, and political liberalism. Since the initial regression model for African Americans, Hispanics, Asian Americans, and Native Americans was affected by heteroscedasticity, weighted least squares was employed using the percentage of the group in the population as the weighting variable (Koutsoyiannis 1977, 188).[5] For estimating the model for women, ordinary least squares regression was used.

Explaining Employment Variation of Minorities and Women in FmHA Districts

As illustrated in Table 5.3, the model employed in this analysis accounts for 77 percent of the variance in African-American FmHA employment. Seven of the variables are statistically significant: African-American population, African-American education, southern region, midwestern region, district office size, state office representation, and funding. For each percentage point increase in total African-American population, African-American representation increases by .08 percentage points. As expected, African-American education, presence of African Americans in the state office, and funding positively affect the percentage of African Americans employed in FmHA districts, while the size of the district office is negatively related to the percentage of positions held by African Americans. The results suggest that African-Americans in higher organizational positions are able to create opportunities for other African Americans in field offices. Compared to districts in the northeast, the findings suggest that African Americans are better represented in the south and midwest. Finally, neither political representation of African Americans nor political ideology of the political representative is related to bureaucratic representation.

An examination of Table 5.4 reveals that 8 variables are significant predictors of Hispanic representation in FmHA districts. Overall, the set of independent variables can explain 54 percent of the variance in Hispanic representation. As was the case for African Americans, regional factors provide the dominant explanation of the variation in employment patterns. The coefficients for the southern, midwestern, and western regional variables are 1.64, 2.49, and 5.98, respectively. Consistent with previous research on Hispanic employment and the

Table 5.3

Percentage of African Americans Employed in FmHA Districts
Estimated with Weighted Least Squares

Independent Variables	Unstandardized Coefficient	Standard Error	Standardized Coefficient
Demographic factors			
African-American population	.08*	.04	.10
% African Americans with High School Degree	.06**	.02	.09
Total population	2.33^{-9}	1.90^{-7}	.00
Economic factors			
Unemployment rate	.15	.10	.05
Region			
South	11.80***	.84	.64
Midwest	5.26***	.54	.39
West	.58	.57	.04
Organizational factors			
Size of district office	−.07**	.02	.12
African American in state director's office	2.14***	.27	.30
Funding for FY 1993	1.17^{-8}*	.00	.08
Political factors			
African American in U.S. House of Representatives	−.90	1.10	.03
Political liberalism	−.01	.01	.05

$R^2 = .77$
Adjusted $R^2 = .76$
$F = 66.75$***
Number of Cases = 246

* significant at .05
** significant at .01
*** significant at .0001

findings presented for African Americans, the size of the Hispanic population exerts a significant and positive impact on employment outcomes in FmHA districts. However, contrary to expectation, districts located in larger rural areas have significantly fewer Hispanic employees. As opposed to the equation presented for African Americans, neither district office size nor the presence of Hispanics in the state director's office are significant predictors of employment. In fact, interminority competition is the only significant organizational factor that emerges in this equation. The analysis indicates that Hispanic employment decreases as African-American representation increases,

Table 5.4

Percentage of Hispanics Employed in FmHA Districts
Estimated with Weighted Least Squares

Independent Variables	Unstandardized Coefficient	Standard Error	Standardized Coefficient
Demographic factors			
Hispanic population	.27***	.06	.36
% Hispanics with high school degree	−.02	.03	.03
Total population	−4.98⁻⁷**	2.00⁻⁷	.15
Economic factors			
Unemployment rate	.15	.10	.08
Region			
South	1.64*	.84	.22
Midwest	2.49**	.59	.30
West	5.98***	1.25	.38
Organizational factors			
Size of district office	−.02	.02	.04
Hispanics in state director's office	−.20	.96	.02
African-American district employees	−.10**	.04	.21
Funding for FY 1993	3.36⁻⁹	.00	.03
Political factors			
Hispanic in U.S. House of Representatives	5.04*	2.25	.15
Political liberalism	.02*	.01	.11

$R^2 = .54$
Adjusted $R^2 = .51$
$F = 18.41^{***}$
Number of Cases = 246

* significant at .05
** significant at .01
*** significant at .0001

suggesting that Hispanics compete with African Americans for FmHA employment opportunities. The most striking difference between the findings for African Americans and Hispanics is that both political factors are significantly related to Hispanic representation. The employment of Hispanics increases by 5.04 percentage points in districts with a Hispanic congressional representative.

The model presented in Table 5.5 explains 65 percent of the variance in Asian-American FmHA employment. The three most important factors in explaining Asian-American representation are Asian-American

Table 5.5

Percentage of Asian Americans Employed in FmHA Districts
Estimated with Weighted Least Squares

Independent Variables	Unstandardized Coefficient	Standard Error	Standardized Coefficient
Demographic factors			
Asian-American population	.75***	.06	.70
% Asian Americans with high school degree	.00	.01	.01
Total population	-3.46^{-7}***	6.00^{-8}	.25
Economic factors			
Unemployment rate	.01	.03	.01
Region			
South	.22	.28	.06
Midwest	−.17	.20	.05
West	−.46	.24	.10
Organizational factors			
Size of district office	−.01	.01	.03
Asian Americans in state director's office	4.71***	.57	.36
African-American district employees	−.02	.01	.10
Funding for FY 1993	8.82^{-9}***	.00	.22
Political factors			
Asian American in U.S. House of Representatives	−2.36	1.72	.07
Political liberalism	.00	.00	.04

$R^2 = .65$
Adjusted $R^2 = .63$
$F = 32.54$***
Number of Cases = 246

*significant at .05
**significant at .01
***significant at .0001

population, Asian-American representation among the state director's personnel, and funding levels. The coefficients for these variables are 0.75, 4.71, and 8.82^{-9}, respectively. Surprisingly, but consistent with the findings for Hispanics, a negative relationship is noted for total population. Although the direction of the relationship is negative, the size of the African-American work force does not have a significant impact on Asian-American job success. Economic factors, as measured by region and unemployment, exert no impact on the variation in

Table 5.6

Percentage of Native Americans Employed in FmHA Districts
Estimated with Weighted Least Squares

Independent Variables	Unstandardized Coefficient	Standard Error	Standardized Coefficient
Demographic factors			
Native American population	.20**	.07	.18
% Native Americans with high school degree	.00	.01	.01
Total population	-9.27^{-8}	7.00^{-8}	.09
Economic factors			
Unemployment rate	.09	.06	.10
Region			
South	−.02	.44	.01
Midwest	.53	.34	.11
West	−.15	.43	.03
Organizational factors			
Size of district office	−.02	.01	.08
Native Americans in state director's office	2.87***	.61	.29
African-American district employees	−.06**	.02	.25
Funding for FY 1993	-8.10^{-9}*	.00	.15
Political factors[1]			
Political liberalism	.00	.00	.02

$R^2 = .26$
Adjusted $R^2 = .23$
$F = 6.98$***
Number of Cases = 246

[1]There were no Native American U.S. representatives in the 103rd Congress.
  * significant at .05
 ** significant at .01
*** significant at .0001

Asian-American employment levels. Whereas both the identity and ideology of elected officials were important determinants of Hispanic employment, neither Asian-American political representation nor ideology results in more job opportunities for Asian Americans.

The ability of the independent variables taken together to explain employment variation is lower for Native Americans ($R^2 = .26$) than it is for African Americans, Hispanics, and Asian Americans (see Table 5.6). The presence of Native Americans in the state office contributes the most of any variable to an explanation of Native American representation. Similar to the findings for Hispanics, Native American employment is negatively related to African-American employment. The success of African Americans reduces the probability that Native Americans will attain positions. Funding also has a significant impact on Native American employment, but not in the predicted direction. One possible explanation is that offices with more resources may operate outreach programs and provide training and educational opportunities that are more accessible to African Americans as they have been denied employment opportunities and program benefits in the past. The variables measuring unemployment and region demonstrate no significant effects, suggesting that these factors are not critical in determining Native American representation.

Compared to the results presented for racial and ethnic minorities, the model is less successful in explaining gender representation (R^2 = .23). For each racial and ethnic minority group examined, group population was meaningful in the determination of group employment. However, these results suggest that female population size is not an important predictor of female representation in FmHA districts. As shown in Table 5.7, only five variables are statistically significant. Female representation varies between regions; women are better represented in the south and midwest. The coefficients for these variables are .23 and .25, respectively. Other FmHA employment characteristics are important in explaining female employment patterns. The findings suggest that women obtain a larger share of positions when more women work in the state director's office and when fewer African Americans are employed. Moreover, women fare better in districts represented by a woman in Congress.

Summary

In summary, the model is most effective in predicting African-American, Hispanic, and Asian-American employment (R^2 = .77, .54, and .65, respectively). The amount of explained variation is considerably smaller with an R^2 of .26 for Native Americans and an R^2 of .23 for women. However, the results converge to suggest several factors that contribute to employment across different groups. Previously, studies have consistently found racial and ethnic group population size to be the primary determinant of municipal employment. The results of this research confirm the general importance of group population, but it is

Table 5.7

Percentage of Women Employed in FmHA Districts

Independent Variables	Unstandardized Coefficient	Standard Error	Standardized Coefficient
Demographic factors			
Female population	.01	.02	.05
Total population	9.30^{-9}	1.00^{-7}	.07
Economic factors			
Unemployment rate	.01	.01	.06
Region			
South	$.23^{**}$	.06	.43
Midwest	$.25^{***}$	.05	.44
West	.00	.05	.01
Organizational factors			
Size of district office	−.001	.00	.06
Women in state director's office	$.04^{***}$	.01	.37
African-American district			
employees	$-.02^{***}$	.00	.51
Funding for FY 1993	-2.38^{-11}	.00	.01
Political factors			
Woman in U.S. House of			
Representatives	$.11^{**}$	.04	.19
Political liberalism	.00	.00	.10

$R^2 = .23$
Adjusted $R^2 = .19$
$F = 5.80^{***}$
Number of Cases = 246

[*]significant at .05
[**]significant at .01
[***]significant at .0001

the dominant predictor only for Asian Americans. Other factors were more important in predicting FmHA employment rates of African Americans, Hispanics, Native Americans, and women. The most visible groups, African Americans, Hispanics, and women, tended to secure more jobs in FmHA districts located in the south and the midwest. For three out of the four groups examined (Hispanics, Native Americans, and women), where African Americans gained a larger share of jobs, they did so at the expense of other groups. While these findings are limited to a single agency, they suggest that interminority group competition exists and has negative consequences for the employment of underrepresented groups.

Of particular importance is the finding in all but one case that more positions are available to a group when other group members work in the state director's office. This suggests that FmHA state offices that employ women and minorities create an environment or culture that encourages the utilization of minorities and women in district offices. The impact may be direct by setting policy or establishing hiring practices that facilitate minority and gender entry, or it may be indirect, resulting from the example of minorities and women working in higher-level agency positions.

The next section moves beyond passive representation and the explanation of employment variations to examine the linkages between passive and active representation. In other words, does representation of African Americans, Hispanics, Asian Americans, Native Americans, and women in districts have an impact on policy outputs affecting African Americans, Hispanics, Asian Americans, Native Americans, and females residing in the district?

Active Representation in FmHA Districts

When decision-making behavior on the part of a particular group of public employees affects systematically the resource allocation to that community, active representation is believed to be occurring (Meier and Stewart 1992; Meier 1993a; Hindera 1993a, 1993b). For example, Meier and Stewart (1992) found that school districts with higher proportions of African-American teachers enrolled higher percentages of African-American students in gifted courses. Because county supervisors are responsible for awarding rural housing loans, this research focuses on whether FmHA county supervisors engage in active representation. Specifically, it looks at the impact of passive representation on the percentage of rural housing loan eligibility determinations awarded to racial and ethnic minorities and women. Figure 5.2 summarizes the influences hypothesized to affect the loan eligibility determinations.

Identifying Variables Possibly Associated with Active Representation

Table 5.8 summarizes the operational definitions of the dependent and independent variables used in subsequent analyses. The dependent variable or the allocational decision providing a focus for the research

Figure 5.2. **Active Representation Within the FmHA**

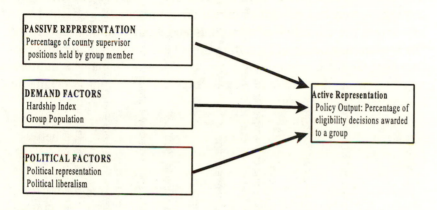

is the loan eligibility determination made by county supervisors. This is operationally defined as the percentage of eligibility determinations in a district favoring specific racial, ethnic, or gender groups.

Passive Representation

Group Employment. The independent variable of primary interest is passive representation of county supervisors in FY 1993. Since the authority to approve a loan belongs to FmHA county supervisors, passive representation is measured as the percentage of county supervisor positions in a district held by members of the specified racial, ethnic, or gender group. The central hypothesis to be examined is whether passive representation of the specified group will be positively correlated with the percentage of eligibility decisions favoring that group.

Demand Factors

In order for inferences regarding the impact of passive representation on policy outputs to be valid, this study will attempt to control statistically for factors other than race or ethnicity of FmHA county supervisors that may reasonably be expected to influence the proportion of eligibility decisions favoring selected groups. The selection of control variables depends, of course, on the research setting used. In an exami-

Table 5.8

Operational Definitions of Dependent and Independent Variables

Dependent Variable: Percentage of Fiscal Year (FY) 1993 eligibility determinations in a district favoring a particular group (African Americans, Hispanics, Native Americans, Asians, and women).

Independent Variable 1: Percentage of county supervisor positions in each district held by a particular group.

Independent Variable 2: Area Hardship Index comprised of:

Poverty: Percentage of selected groups living in poverty in 1990

Unemployment: Percentage of selected group's labor force that is unemployed in 1990

Dependency: Percentage of selected group's population that is less than 18 or over 64 years of age in 1990

Education: Percentage of selected group's population 25 years of age or more with less than a twelfth-grade education in 1990

Income Level: Per capita income of selected group in 1990

Independent Variable 3: Percentage of population comprised of members of selected group in 1990

Independent Variable 4: *Political Representation.* The variable is dichotomous. Districts represented by a group member in the U.S. House of Representatives are coded 1.

Independent Variable 5: *Political Ideology.* 1993 Americans for Democratic Action (ADA) rating for the FmHA district's House of Representatives member. The index is scaled from 0 (conservative) to 100 (liberal). When more than one member of the House of Representatives represents the district's population, a weighted ideology index is constructed by weighting each member's rating relative to the proportion of the district's population he or she represents, and summing the proportional ratings.

nation of the link between passive and active representation in district EEOC offices, Hindera (1993a) controlled for the proportion of a demographic group within the labor pool, city size, and political ideology of the House delegation representing the area in which the district office was located. In studies of educational bureaucracies, scholars controlled for the percentage of group population over age twenty-five with a high school diploma, the percentage of Anglo residents in poverty (to represent Anglo social class), and the ratio of Latino to Anglo personal income (expressed as a percentage) (Meier 1993a; Meier and Stewart 1991; Meier, Stewart, and England 1989). These controls were included to ensure that the relationship found between employment and policy outcomes and outputs did not reflect simply the social class disadvantages of the group or the political resources available to the group.

Hardship Index. In the present study, similar factors are likely to affect the demand for housing loans and eligibility decisions made by county supervisors. For example, because the Rural Housing Loans program targets moderate-income to very-low-income people, areas with more low-income residents of a particular group are likely to place more demand on the program than other areas. The proportion of applications filed by members of a specific group will affect the percentage of eligibility determinations favoring that group. However, the FmHA was unable to provide nationwide information on the number of applications received in each district. Instead, this study will use district characteristics, such as percentage of a group living in the district and percentage of a group living below the poverty line, to control for demand.

Due to the high intercorrelation of area characteristics that may affect the demand for rural housing loans, such as unemployment, income level, and poverty, this study used an index developed by the Brookings Institution to gauge area hardship to mitigate problems of multicollinearity. Five measures available from the 1990 census constitute the hardship index: poverty, unemployment, dependency, education and income level (see Table 5.8 for a more detailed exploration).[6]

Each of these ratios was standardized to give equal weight to each of these comparative measures and then summed to compute the hardship index (see Nathan and Adams 1976, 1989; O'Sullivan and Rassel 1995).[7] The higher a group's hardship index, the more adverse a group's economic situation is in an area. A particular group's demand for low-income rural housing loans will be higher in areas where that group faces more economic adversity. Therefore, FmHA districts are likely to classify a higher percentage of members of a specific group as eligible in areas in which that group is economically depressed.

Group Population. The proportion of eligibility decisions awarded to a particular group will also be associated with the population size of that group within the district. Three different reasons may account for such a relationship. First, minorities in areas with larger shares of minority residents have access to more political resources; that is, they control a larger share of votes and, as a result, should have more influence over policy implementation. Second, county offices located in districts with larger populations of a group are more likely to employ individuals from that group. Third, merely having a larger proportion of a group residing in a district should increase the probability of receiving more applications from that group. As a result, the number of loan determinations awarded to the group in these areas is likely to exceed the number awarded in areas with fewer group residents. Given these three reasons, it is necessary to also control for the population of a particular group in the district.

Political Factors

Political Representation. Previous studies of active representation have not controlled for the influence of elected officials on the distribution of program resources. As indicated above, municipal employment research has documented that representation of minorities in elected positions is associated with minority bureaucratic representation. Since previous research has shown that representation of elected officials is an important determinant of employment policy, this model hypothesizes that county supervisors will allocate more FmHA program resources to minorities and women when their congressperson is a minority or a woman.

Political Ideology. In addition to the demographic characteristics of elected officials, elected officials' political ideology may be an important factor in determining resource allocations. Several authors have claimed that both senators and members of Congress can influence the implementation of federal policy within their respective districts (Dodd and Schott 1979; Ripley and Franklin 1991). According to John Scholz, Jim Twombly, and Barbara Headrick (1991), partisan activities of elected officials systemically influence bureaucratic behaviors. They learned that county, state, and federal elected officials influenced OSHA enforcement in New York. At the county level, liberal legislators were associated with more active enforcement of OSHA regulations. John Chubb (1985) also found that liberal representatives were more inclined to vigorously oversee policies that assisted the disadvantaged because the disadvantaged were a more important part of their constituency. Because the Rural Housing Loans program is redistributive in nature, and because it may be argued that liberal members of Congress will be fundamentally predisposed toward support for policies on behalf of low-income citizens, while conservative members will tend to not support redistributive policy decisions, it is expected that as the liberalism of the district representatives increases, the proportion of loan eligibility decisions favoring minorities in a district will also increase. Consequently, subsequent analysis will control for the ideology of House delegates elected in the district regions.

As illustrated in Figure 5.2 (page 99), the percentage of eligibility decisions awarded to a group is modeled as a function of group employment, the needs index of that group, the group's population size, political representation of the group in Congress, and the political ideology of congressional representatives. The models were estimated with weighted least squares, using the percentage of the group in the population as the weighting variable.[8]

Explaining the Allocation of FmHA Program Resources

The multivariate analysis of loans awarded to African Americans is shown in Table 5.9. The relationship between the percentage of African-American supervisors and the percentage of eligibility decisions favoring African Americans is positive, as expected. A one percentage point increase in African-American supervisors is associated with a 1.06 percentage point increase in eligibility decisions favoring African Americans. Similarly, district population of African Americans is associated with a higher percentage of loan eligibility decisions favoring the African-American community. Both relationships are strongly significant. The relationships between eligibility determinations favoring African Americans and the three other control variables—hardship

Table 5.9

Impact of Passive Representation on the Percentage of Eligibility Determinations Awarded to African Americans
Estimated with Weighted Least Squares

Independent Variables	Unstandardized Coefficient	Standard Error	Standardized Coefficient
Passive Representation			
African-American supervisors	1.06***	.14	.39
Demand Factors			
African-American hardship index	−.02	.24	.01
African-American population	1.71***	.34	.51
Political Factors			
African-American in U.S.			
House of Representatives	.28	4.86	.00
Political liberalism	−.01	.03	.01

$$R^2 = .68$$
Adjusted $R^2 = .67$
$$F = 102.03^{***}$$
Number of Cases = 246

* significant at .05
* significant at .01
*** significant at .0001

index, political representation, and political liberalism—are not statistically significant in this model. Overall, the model accounts for 68 percent of the variance in the percentage of eligibility decisions favoring African Americans. This study provides substantial evidence that districts with higher percentages of African-American supervisors allocate more FmHA resources to African-American citizens. A U.S. Civil Rights Commission report (1982, 91) suggested that perceived and actual program inequities within the FmHA may be due, in part, to the low percentage of minorities employed in decision-making positions. Although this study does not explicitly examine inequities in program resource distribution between African-American and Caucasian citizens, it does suggest that increasing the share of African Americans employed in key decision-making positions is a real and viable means of combating and countering historic biases within the agency.

Like the Black population, Hispanics represent a large, visible minority who have experienced discrimination (Massey 1979; Darden 1986; Bean and Tienda 1987; Hraba 1994). Although the number of

Table 5.10

Impact of Passive Representation on the Percentage of Eligibility Determinations Awarded to Hispanics
Estimated with Weighted Least Squares

Independent Variables	Unstandardized Coefficient	Standard Error	Standardized Coefficient
Passive Representation			
Hispanic supervisors	.93***	.04	.77
Demand Factors			
Hispanic hardship index	.83*	.37	.37
Hispanic population	−.39	.37	.17
Political Factors			
Hispanic in U.S. House of Representatives	5.08	4.11	.05
Political liberalism	−.01	.02	.02

$$R^2 = .76$$
$$\text{Adjusted } R^2 = .76$$
$$F = 152.63***$$
Number of Cases = 246

* significant at .05
** significant at .01
*** significant at .0001

Blacks immigrating to the United States has increased over the last three decades, Hispanics are immigrating at higher rates, and the U.S. Census Bureau estimates that by the year 2080, Hispanics will be the largest minority group (Kivisto 1995, 102). The attitudes and values of Hispanics and other racial and ethnic groups may differ depending on their native country, culture, length of time they have resided in the United States, areas of the United States in which they have lived, and their political experiences (Meier 1993b; Meier and Stewart 1991). Although a few studies have looked at different Hispanic groups, others have treated Hispanics as a single group (Meier and Stewart 1992; Meier 1993b; Hindera 1993a, 1993b). Because I was unable to obtain program and personnel data that would allow me to examine different Hispanic groups, this analysis focuses on Hispanics as a single group.[9]

As Table 5.10 shows, Hispanic FmHA employment and economic hardship of Hispanics exert a statistically significant influence on eligibility decisions favoring Hispanics, while Hispanic population, political representation, and political liberalism prove unimportant statistically in predicting eligibility decisions. The model explains 76

Table 5.11

Impact of Passive Representation on the Percentage of Eligibility Determinations Awarded to Asian Americans
Estimated with Weighted Least Squares

Independent Variables	Unstandardized Coefficient	Standard Error	Standardized Coefficient
Passive Representation			
Asian-American supervisors	1.42***	.06	.82
Demand Factors			
Asian-American hardship index	.00	.05	.00
Asian-American population	.34	.18	.10
Political Factors			
Asian-American in U.S.			
House of Representatives	−6.00	4.83	.06
Political liberalism	.00	.01	.01

$$R^2 = .71$$
$$\text{Adjusted } R^2 = .71$$
$$F = 119.79^{***}$$
$$\text{Number of Cases} = 246$$

* significant at .05
** significant at .01
*** significant at .0001

percent of the variance in the dependent variable. These results also demonstrate the strength of the relationship between employment patterns and policy outputs.

Like African Americans and Hispanics, the relationship between passive and active representation holds for Asian Americans (see Table 5.11). In other words, FmHA districts that employed more Asian Americans awarded a larger percentage of eligibility decisions to Asian Americans. None of the control variables in this model are statistically significant. Overall, the independent variables account for 71 percent of the variation in the number of eligibility decisions favoring Asian Americans. The results for this model differ from the models for African Americans, Hispanics, and Asian Americans in that neither population nor economic hardship, which are likely to affect the distribution of rural housing loans, are statistically significant.

Several attributes of Asian culture may contribute to these differences. First, many Asian-American groups have built their own ethnic subeconomies and are inclined to take care of, help, and protect other

Asian Americans and Asian immigrants (Hraba 1994). Asian Americans living in FmHA districts with large Asian populations may have more access to private capital in the Asian community, and therefore may not be as inclined to pursue government-backed lending sources. Moreover, because the Asian culture values and encourages helping others within the community, Asians may be more comfortable pursuing government-backed loans when the decision maker is Asian.

The widespread belief that Asians in the United States are a model minority who are not as in need of government assistance may also contribute to the insignificant findings for the two demand factors (Sue 1994).

> Asian Americans are considered by the dominant group as "successful" and "problem free" and not in need of social programmes designed to benefit disadvantaged minorities such as blacks and Mexican Americans. . . . A number of cases of official inattention to the problems and needs of Asian Americans have already been reported in public documents and scholarly publications. (Hurh and Kim 1989, 528)

There is a tendency within Asian-American culture not to verbalize problems and difficulties; this may in turn reinforce the relatively positive image of Asian Americans (Sue 1989, 1994). However, recent statistics indicate that while the average family income of Asian Americans is slightly higher than that of Caucasians, the poverty rate of Asian Americans is nearly twice that of Caucasians (O'Hare and Felt 1991). Because Asian Americans are viewed as a model minority and are not prone to ask for government assistance, the needs and problems of disadvantaged Asian Americans have received little attention from public officials (U.S. Commission on Civil Rights 1980; Hurh and Kim 1989). The results of this study suggest that one means of ensuring that the needs of low-income Asian Americans are considered is to increase Asian-American representation in agencies implementing redistributive programs.

When controlling for hardship of Native Americans, Native American population, and political liberalism, the relationship between percentage of eligibility decisions favoring Native Americans and the percentage of Native Americans serving as county supervisors in the district is not significant (see Table 5.12). The economic hardship of Native Americans served by the district and Native American population in the district

Table 5.12

Impact of Passive Representation on the Percentage of Eligibility Determinations Awarded to Native Americans
Estimated with Weighted Least Squares

Independent Variables	Unstandardized Coefficient	Standard Error	Standardized Coefficient
Passive Representation			
Native American supervisors	−.29	.20	.09
Demand Factors			
Native American hardship index	.60**	.23	.22
Native American population	1.48***	.54	.23
Political Factors[1]			
Political liberalism	−.04	.03	.08

R^2 = .16
Adjusted R^2 = .14
F = 11.29***
Number of Cases = 246

[1]There were no Native American U.S. representatives in the 103rd Congress.
* significant at .05
** significant at .01
*** significant at .0001

are statistically significant in the model. A 1.0 percentage point increase in Native American population is associated with a 1.48 percentage point increase in eligibility decisions favoring Native Americans. This model explains only 16 percent of the variance in the percentage of eligibility decisions favoring Native Americans.

To derive a better understanding of the insignificant linkage between passive and active representation of Native Americans, I contacted several county supervisors serving areas with large concentrations of Native Americans. According to an official with the FmHA (personal interview with author 1995), in rural areas with large concentrations of Native Americans, most Native Americans live on tribal reservations that often operate tribal housing authorities. Although located in rural areas, these authorities oversee and administer housing loans funded by HUD (personal interview with author 1995). Because of other low-income government-funding options, fewer Native Americans may apply for FmHA rural housing loans. Thus, the share of loans awarded to Native Americans may be lower than expected because districts may receive fewer applications than suggested by the population and economic conditions of Native Americans living in the district. This study, however, cannot account directly for the number of applications received from Native Americans.

Table 5.13 presents the results of the analysis for women. None of the predicted relationships are significant. The model offers no support for the linkage between passive and active representation for women in this particular policy arena. That is, districts with higher shares of female county supervisors did not award more eligibility determinations favoring females. Based on the literature, housing appears to be a salient issue for women as they have historically had trouble gaining credit approval from lending institutions (Birch 1985, 1989; Conway, Ahern, and Steuernagel 1995; Gelb and Palley 1982; Stegman 1985). In the mid-1970s, women activists lobbied and won on several important points regarding women and credit discrimination (Gelb and Palley 1982). Eugenie Birch (1989, 99) suggests that improving the purchasing power of female heads of households could be accomplished by increasing access to programs that "reduce the costs of construction, rehabilitation, and home purchase." Clearly, the Rural Housing Loans program is one means of increasing access to low-income women. In addition to this being an important issue for women, there is significant variation in the employment of women and percentage of eligibility decisions favoring women in districts. Nevertheless, this model does not explain any of the variation in the percentage of eligibility decisions favoring women. This study is not able to examine the relationship for minority and nonminority women as the data were not available from the FmHA. A comparison of the results for minority and nonminority women would have provided insight about the interactive effects of gender and race. Such an analysis might have revealed that this was an important issue for minority women, but not for white women.

The findings for women, however, are not inconsistent with previous research examining passive and active representation for women. Hindera's work (1993a) tested the linkage between female representation in the EEOC and the number of discrimination complaints filed on behalf of women. Contrary to expectations, Hindera found that white females filed significantly fewer complaints on behalf of women and that the relationship between employment of African-American females and the number of complaints filed on behalf of women was not significant. This study's findings indicate that for this particular pro-

Table 5.13

**Impact of Passive Representation on the Percentage of Eligibility
Determinations Awarded to Women**
Estimated with Weighted Least Squares

Independent Variables	Unstandardized Coefficient	Standard Error	Standardized Coefficient
Passive Representation			
Female supervisors	.01	.14	.00
Demand Factors			
Female hardship index	−.11	.14	.06
Female population	2.48	2.74	.07
Political Factors			
Woman in U.S. House of			
Representatives	−2.21	5.28	.03
Political liberalism	− .11	.09	.08

$R^2 = .01$
Adjusted $R^2 = .00$
$F = .55$
Number of Cases = 246

[*] significant at .05
[**] significant at .01
[***] significant at .0001

gram, female administrators do not award a larger share of resources to females than male county supervisors. However, these same female administrators may be inclined to pursue other policies that have obvious connections to female concerns, such as child care, the Equal Rights Amendment (ERA), pregnancy/disability benefits, job sharing, and pay equity (Hale and Branch 1992; Hale and Kelly 1989a, 1989b; Hale, Kelly, and Burgess 1989). Alternatively, the FmHA may have socialized female county supervisors in a manner that does not support or encourage decisions that actively represent the interests of other women.

The statistically significant relationships between African-American, Hispanic, and Asian-American group representation and the percentage of eligibility decisions favoring those groups provide evidence in support of the central hypothesis of this study, i.e., that passive representation of a particular group in the government bureaucracy helps to determine the resources allocated to that group of citizens. The race, ethnicity, gender, and political ideology of members of Congress serving the districts does not significantly influence loan decisions on behalf of racial and ethnic minorities. FmHA districts may be too far removed geographically and organizationally to be influenced significantly by their congressional representatives. A case study of organizational communications in the FmHA published in 1988 reported that "county supervisors had to figure out the limits within which they could act. . . . They felt removed from Washington and said so" (Wyatt and Phillips 1988, 98).

Conclusions

This chapter examined the passive representation, or employment, of ethnic and racial minorities and women, and its relationship to active representation. The first half of the chapter looked at factors that have been suggested to explain employment variation among African Americans, Hispanics, Asian Americans, Native Americans, and women. Some interesting patterns emerge from the research. As with studies of municipal employment, group population was an important determinant of employment of racial and ethnic minorities in FmHA districts. However, it was not a significant predictor of female representation. The findings reveal that when African Americans gain positions, they do so at the expense of Hispanics, Native Americans, and women. This suggests that as African-American employment success increases, competition between African Americans and other groups may result. Another important organizational factor that consistently had an impact on district employment was representation within the state director's office. Minorities and women fared better when minorities and women were represented in the state director's office. As suggested earlier, the state director has the authority for setting vision and creating an environment that may encourage and facilitate practices that increase minority and gender representation. Although political representation was not consistently important across all five groups, it was a significant predictor of Hispanic and female employment patterns. This study provides further insights into the conditions under which minorities and women succeed in federal employment.

This research also adds to the growing body of literature on the relationship between passive and active representation by testing it in a setting that is unique to those previously studied. In all but one case, the ethnic or racial composition of the FmHA district affects the proportion of eligibility decisions awarded to a minority group. These findings reinforce the notion that the representativeness of the bureaucracy can affect bureaucratic responsiveness to identifiable segments of the population. The results of this study are particularly important because active representation is found in an agency whose primary mission does not emphasize minority issues, that historically has employed low percentages of minorities, and that has implemented policies that have adversely affected minorities. In addition to examining active representation in a different policy setting, this research extends previous studies by examining this relationship for Asian Americans and Native Americans.

Notes

1. In total there are 252 FmHA district offices, of which six have been excluded from the analysis. The districts serving residents of Puerto Rico, the Virgin Islands, Guam, American Samoa, and the Commonwealth of the Northern Mariana Islands are not included in the analysis.

2. The county supervisor is the top-level position within each office, and the lower-level positions report directly to the county supervisor. Although part of the county supervisor's job includes supervision of these employees, the position is still considered street-level as the county supervisor works directly with potential clients in processing loan applications.

3. The relationship may be complicated by an interaction between political ideology and political representation. For example, areas represented by a liberal Hispanic in Congress might be more likely to employ Hispanics than areas represented by a conservative Hispanic.

4. For example, suppose that two House delegates represent residents from counties comprising FmHA district office X. Delegate A represents 60 percent of the district's population, and Delegate B represents the remaining 40 percent. Delegate A received a 1993 ADA rating of 90, and Delegate B received a rating of 85. The weighted indexed is calculated as follows:

| Proportion of the district population represented by Delegate A | × | ADA rating for Delegate A | + | Proportion of the district population represented by Delegate B | × | ADA rating for Delegate B |

or $(90 \times .60) + (85 \times .40) = 88$.

The ideology index for district X is 88.

5. White's statistical procedure was used to test for heteroscedasticity in the regression model for each group (Pindyck and Rubinfeld 1991). For African Americans, Hispanics, Asian Americans, and Native Americans, the error variances varied with the percentage of the group residing in the area.

6. Because per capita income ranges from more economic hardship to less economic hardship, and the rest of the indicators range from less economic hardship to more economic hardship, the per capita income scale was reversed. This was done by subtracting 100 from the standardized per capita income score and multiplying it by negative one.

7. The following formula was applied to each of the hardship indicators to standardize them:

$$X = \left(\frac{Y - Y_{min}}{Y_{max} - Y_{min}} \right) 100$$

where:

X = standardized ratio to be created

Y = variable calculated from census data

Y_{max} = maximum value of Y

Y_{min} = minimum value of Y.

The standardized values indicate where each district office is on a continuum of hardship ranging from the "worst" district to the "best" district. Accordingly, the ratio for each hardship indicator ranges from a value of 0 (the district with the lowest rating) to 100 (the district with the highest rating). The standardized indicators were summed and then divided by six. The ranges of the hardship indexes are as follows: African Americans from 1.11 to 84.65; Hispanics from .08 to 95.09; Asian Americans from 1.17 to 88.64; and Native Americans from 2.09 to 78.28. For each of the indexes constructed, the individual items correlated with the index at the .80 level or higher.

8. For each group, I used White's statistical procedure to test for heteroscedasticity in the regression model (Pindyck and Rubinfeld 1991). For each group, the variance in the error term varied with the explanatory variable, percentage of the group in the population. Weighted least squares was employed, using the percentage of the group in the population as the weighting variable, to estimate the equations (Koutsoyiannis 1977, 188).

9. Meier and Stewart (1991) analyzed the representation of Mexican Americans, Puerto Ricans, and Cuban Americans in selected school districts.

6

Understanding the Process of Active Representation: Developing and Testing a Model of Administrative Behavior

Chapter 5 examined the relationship between passive representation of African Americans, Hispanics, Asians, Native Americans, and women and policy outputs benefiting those groups in FmHA districts. A significant relationship was found for three out of the four minority groups. The task in this chapter is to better understand the process of active representation by focusing on the individual administrator rather than the districts. The chapter examines factors that may lead an administrator to assume a minority advocacy or representative role, and how this role perception affects an individual's behavior. The chapter builds an integrative model of active representative behavior, and tests it empirically in a sample of county supervisors of the Farmers Home Administration (FmHA) employed in the southern region of the United States.[1]

A Model of Representative Role and Administrative Behavior

Figure 6.1 presents the integrative model of the formation of an advocacy or representative role perception among public administrators and its manifestation in active representative behavior, that is, actions and decisions taken by them reflecting the interests of minority groups. The

Figure 6.1. Linkages in the Concept of Representative Bureaucracy

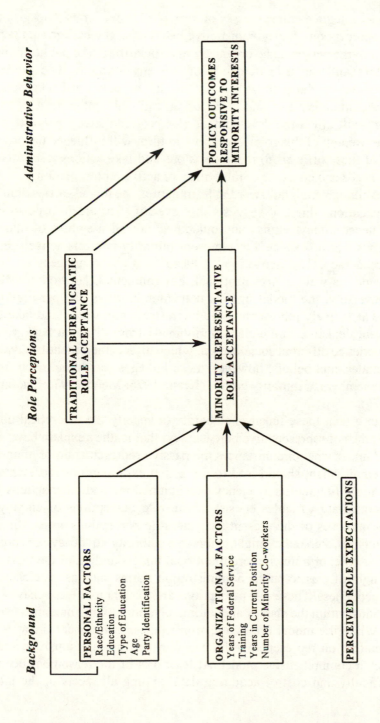

model integrates three classes of variables: bureaucrats' backgrounds, role perceptions, and administrative behaviors. The background factors refer to the personal and organizational socialization of public administrators and the role demands of the environment. The model is grounded on the premise that factors in the personal background of public administrators and in the organizational context in which they work will affect the development of a representative role perception. The strength of this role perception, in turn, will influence the proclivity of these officials to make decisions and take actions responsive to the needs and concerns of minorities, or active representation.

Although straightforward in formulation, the model carries dramatic implications. First, it suggests that even if they are in a position to influence policy outputs and outcomes, not all members of minority groups can be expected to represent minority interests actively in the bureaucracy. The activation of these views is contingent on background, as well as organizational, environmental, and role variables. Conversely, the model implies that nonminorities can perceive their role as actively representing the interests of minorities, and take congruent decisions and actions. Individuals from different backgrounds experience different socialization, which affects their identities, values, attitudes, and beliefs; however, these linkages should be much firmer for members of minority groups (Kranz 1976; Meier 1993c; Thompson 1976).

In effect, these linkages elaborate or specify the theoretical underpinnings of representative bureaucracy; that is, they explain how, why, and under what circumstances the passive representation of minorities in employment should lead to the active expression or representation of minority interests in agency decision making and other actions. The intermediate variables consist of the role perceptions of employees. For purposes of the present analysis, role perceptions are confined to two types. Personnel might embrace a minority advocacy or representative role, or a much more traditional understanding of the work role in light of classic public administration norms such as efficiency and effectiveness. These role perceptions are thought to affect behavior and actions within the agency and, ultimately, outputs and outcomes.

While the model draws attention to these component linkages, the literature on representative bureaucracy has not previously examined such a comprehensive model. At least part of the reason has been the difficulty and cost of acquiring data tapping all facets of the model, including information on the personal background and role perceptions of individual administrators, as well as socialization to the agency and policy outputs. As explained below, the present study assembles this information for agency decision makers who exercise substantial discretion in a policy domain crucial to minority interests—housing loans.

Development of a Representative Role

The development of a minority representative or advocacy role is central to the model. Roles are described as sets of expected behaviors to be performed by a person occupying a particular position (Kahn, Wolfe, Quinn, and Snoek 1964; Turner 1956; Widmer 1993). Role expectations or demands are conveyed by other stakeholders, both verbally and nonverbally, as well as expressed formally through job descriptions, training, and other avenues of socialization. In addition to these "sent" roles, consisting of expectations and pressures that are communicated by stakeholders, there is also a "received" role, consisting of an individual's perceptions of what was sent (Kahn, Wolfe, Quinn, and Snoek 1964; Turner 1956; Widmer 1993). Individuals may encounter multiple role expectations, which can result in cross-pressures and conflicts. Ultimately, according to Kahn, Wolfe, Quinn, and Snoek (1964, 16), "it is the received role, however, which is the immediate influence on . . . behavior and the immediate source of . . . motivation to role performance."

Several scholars have examined organizational and environmental conditions that influence the roles minority administrators assume in public organizations (Henderson 1988; Martinez 1991; McClain and Karnig 1988; Murray et al. 1994). Adam W. Herbert's (1974) classic article, "The Minority Administrator," has had a significant impact on how scholars view the role of minority administrators in public organizations. According to Herbert (1974), minority administrators confront at least six forces that influence minority role perceptions: system demands, traditional role expectations, colleague pressures, community accountability, personal commitment to community, and ambition. Although the article focuses on minority bureaucrats, Herbert (1974) recognizes that many of the role dilemmas encountered confront all administrators regardless of race.

These forces, outlined by Herbert, do not necessarily create the same demands and expectations of administrators. To the extent that demands and expectations differ and contradict one another, the administrator is likely to experience role conflict. Organizations create system demands by rewarding certain behaviors and sanctioning others. For example, employees may be rewarded for "doing as ordered" and may be sanctioned for diverging from standard practices and procedures.

Beyond formal rewards and sanctions, administrators may feel pressure from colleagues to conform to bureaucratic, professional, or informal norms set by other employees (Herbert 1974). Henderson (1988) cautions that underlying norms of behavior in organizations can operate to discourage administrators who openly seek to represent minority interests.

But at the same time, some administrators, especially minorities, may feel an intense sense of responsibility to minority communities. According to Herbert (1974, 561), minority communities want public administrators "who will listen to them, who can communicate with them, who care about them." Albert Karnig and Paula McClain (1988, 151–152) describe the role associated with this behavior as one of a "trustee" of minority interests. Trustees bear responsibility for making a positive difference in policy outcomes for minorities and for increasing their access to the policy process. The trustee role parallels Frederick Mosher's (1982) concept of active representation, which occurs when minority civil servants work to see that the interests and desires of minority groups are represented in policy decisions.

As a result, public administrators may experience cross-pressures to conform to organizational norms emphasizing bureaucratic routine, efficiency, and strict interpretation of rules, while also feeling a need to shape policy decisions responsive to particularized interests. For example, Herbert (1974, 563) maintains that to assume a minority representative role, individuals may have to reject the idea that administrators are and must be "value free and completely neutral," yet he acknowledges that administrators work in bureaucratic settings with established organizational norms, procedures, and reward structures that cannot and should not be ignored. Each individual must decide the relative weights to assign to the various job expectations and demands in conceiving his or her work role. Thomas Martinez (1991) notes that from an institutional or bureaucratic perspective, the concern arises that when administrators work to represent minority interests, their obligations to the general public may be pushed aside, thus threatening principles of administrative neutrality.

According to the model presented in Figure 6.1, four sets of variables affect assumption of a minority representative role: an individual's personal background, organizational socialization, the perceived salience of a traditional bureaucratic role conception emphasizing values such as administrative efficiency in the execution of organizational duties, and the administrator's perception of the role expectations that others in the policy process hold for her or him.

Personal Factors

Race and Ethnicity. The literature on representative bureaucracy has been concerned with race and ethnicity primarily for comparing the composition of the public work force with that of the larger population. The idea that race and ethnicity will help to shape role perceptions is compelling since many important political attitudes are constructed along racial and ethnic lines. Guinier (1994, 137), for example, has argued that "race in this country has defined individual identities, opportunities, frames of reference, and relationships. Where race has been of historical importance and continues to play a significant role, racial-group membership often serves as a political proxy for shared experience and common interests." Murray et al. (1994) confirm the importance of race in public administration. In their survey of minority public administrators, most respondents believed that they should play a strong representational role for minority communities. Earlier work examining policy outcomes has supported the contention that minority employment will further minority policy interests at least with respect to some policy issues. For example, Meier (1993a) and Meier and Stewart (1992) found that the employment of minority public school teachers and principals is associated with fewer disciplinary actions against minority students. Similarly, Hindera (1993a, 1993b) demonstrated that the presence of minority EEOC investigators is positively associated with the percentage of discrimination charges filed on behalf of minorities in EEOC district offices. For the reasons outlined, the model posits that racial and ethnic minorities will be more likely than nonminority administrators to adhere to a minority representative role.

Education. Education is a second personal factor that may influence administrators' role perceptions. Meier (1993c, 26) suggests that "educational institutions, particularly at the post-secondary level, play an important role in the socialization of minorities and women by raising consciousness about the problems facing minorities and women in society." Similarly, this logic could be applied to nonminority individuals. That is, nonminority individuals may also become more sensitized to minority problems as a result of higher education. If so, then administrators with more formal post-secondary education should generally be more likely to assume a minority representative role than those with less education. Only a few studies have examined the relevance of education to representative bureaucracy, however, and empirical findings have been mixed. Dennis Daley (1984) found that state government officials with more formal education were more likely to disapprove of policies for "improving the condition of ethnic minorities and women"; whereas Meier and Nigro (1976) found that federal government executives (GS-16 to GS-18) with more education expressed more support for improving the conditions of minorities. The association between level of education and adherence to a minority representative role is reexamined in the present analysis.

Type of Education. The type of higher education institution attended by an administrator may also influence the individual's perception of work roles. Rosenbloom and Kinnard (1977), for instance, found that minority administrators who had attended historically black colleges believed that they were more effective at facilitating the entry of minorities into high-level positions in the Department of Defense. Historically black colleges and universities may inculcate a shared sense of identity or purpose that carries over into perceived work roles. For this reason, the model hypothesizes that administrators who have attended these schools will be more sensitive to minority interests and will more readily adopt a minority representative role.

Age. Research has also identified age as a significant demographic variable in studies of bureaucratic attitudes (Daley 1984; Meier and Nigro 1976; Rosenbloom and Kinnard 1977). Typically, younger employees have worked for government for shorter periods and therefore have experienced less socialization to organizational norms and values. Moreover, they are not as removed as older employees from their childhood experiences and roots. While age is related to organizational socialization factors, such as years in federal government, it also taps a slightly different dimension (Daley 1984). Individuals of the same age cohort have experienced similar historical events that have shaped their "generation" (e.g., World War II, Vietnam, the civil rights movement, and the Persian Gulf War). These factors complicate the relationship between age and the assumption of a minority advocacy or representative role.

For example, a 1976 study reported evidence that older bureaucrats were less supportive of policies aimed at improving the conditions of minorities (Meier and Nigro 1976). The following year, another study found that younger minority managers felt a stronger responsibility to help other minorities within the field of public administration (Rosenbloom and Kinnard 1977). However, in the 1980s, Daley (1984) found that older administrators were more supportive of a representative bureaucracy and of increasing efforts to achieve this goal. Given that many older administrators in the mid-1990s came to maturity during the time of the civil rights movement and the struggle for racial equality in the 1960s, age is expected to be positively associated with attachment to a minority representative role.

Party Identification. It is also likely that political party identification will be linked to attitudes toward the representation of minority interests. Seymour Martin Lipset (1992) noted that, in recent years, the debate over hiring preferences for minorities has sharply divided the two major political parties, with Republicans generally opposed to such programs while Democrats favor them. Individuals with more liberal political orientations are more likely to support policies that benefit minority groups. Thompson (1978), for example, found that individuals who identified with the Democratic Party were more receptive to hiring minorities. The closer an individual identifies with the Republican Party, the less likely he or she will be to assume a minority representative role.

Organizational Factors

Since socialization is an ongoing learning process that continues once an individual enters an organizational setting, and because agencies can create an environment or culture emphasizing organizational loyalty and commitment, socialization to the organization may weaken the link between the demographic background of administrators and adherence to a minority representative role when the organization's mission or culture does not emphasize minority interests (Meier and Nigro 1976; Romzek and Hendricks 1982). Meier (1993a, 397) suggests that when administrators have spent the time necessary in an organization to attain a position of power, they "often have been subjected to many years of organizational socialization designed to encourage employees to adopt agency-sanctioned attitudes." If those values do not include active representation, individuals who seek to represent minority interests may be pressured to abandon such activity (Meier 1993a). Early studies of representative bureaucracy by Meier (1975) and Meier and Nigro (1976) found that organizational socialization was often a more important predictor of bureaucratic attitudes than were social origins and background characteristics of civil servants.[2]

Three indicators of exposure to organizational socialization are the amount of formal agency training received by the administrator, the length of employment in the current position, and the length of government employment in general. Based on the history and culture of the FmHA, each of these variables is expected to be negatively associated with adherence to a minority representative role. This would not be the case, however, for organizations that socialize members to values consistent with the theory of representative bureaucracy, such as the EEOC. In the empirical analysis, should the hypothesized negative effect of organizational socialization overwhelm the effects of attitudes and values stemming from administrators' personal backgrounds on the assumption of this role, the potential for representative bureaucracy would be weakened substantially. The theory of representative bureaucracy presumes that social background characteristics will be reflected in the work attitudes and behaviors of bureaucrats.

Another aspect of the organizational setting, the presence of minority co-workers in the work environment, may operate to reinforce the minority representative role. Thompson (1976) maintains that bureaucrats will be more likely to engage in active representation of minority interests when they work in close proximity to and interact more frequently with members of minority groups. The employment of several minority employees by an agency may lead to greater comfort and confidence in pursuing policies responsive to minority interests. For this reason, an administrator will be more likely to assume a minority representative role as the number of minority co-workers in the office increases.[3]

Perceived Role Expectations

The role expectations that other actors hold for an administrator will likely influence his or her perceptions concerning proper work roles. These actors include management, colleagues, employee organizations, the general public, the minority community, professional associations, and political officials. The role expectations of other actors do not necessarily coincide with the administrators' own perceptions or goals. Instead, administrators must reconcile the differing expectations of various actors with their own goals and commitments. When administrators perceive that other actors in the policy process expect them to represent minority interests, they may be more inclined to accept the minority representative role (Kahn et al. 1964).

As discussed above, the literature suggests that minority administrators often perceive that they face dual expectations of advocating or representing minority group interests and conforming to more traditional or bureaucratically defined administrative roles (Martinez 1991; Murray et al. 1994). In this situation, administrators may seek a compromise between the two positions in which they still adhere to the minority representative role but not to the same degree as when they experience no cross-pressure (Murray et al. 1994). The analysis below examines the effects of all three sets of perceived role pressures on the assumption of a minority representative role.

Role Perceptions

The way in which an individual conceives of his or her role will affect behavior on the job (Kahn, Wolfe, Quinn, and Snoek 1964; Miller and Wager 1971). Central to the present research is the hypothesis that administrators who perceive of their role as a representative of minority interests are more likely to engage in behaviors that benefit the minority community. Individuals who adhere to more traditional bureaucratic roles are not as likely to undertake such actions: the traditional role emphasizes neutrality, merit, and even-handedness, and will, therefore, likely counter behaviors intended to increase minority access to the policy process. According to Herbert Kaufman (1956, 1060), the essence of neutral competence is the "ability to do the work of the government expertly, and to do it according to explicit, objective standards rather than to personal or party or other obligations and loyalties." Patricia Ingraham and Carolyn Ban (1986) argue that the central values in the traditional view of neutral competence are economy and efficiency.

These two role perceptions are not the antithesis of one another and are not mutually exclusive. An individual who perceives of his or her role as a minority advocate may also value efficiency. As discussed earlier, Murray et al. (1994) found evidence that minority administrators view both of these roles as important. Although the minority advocacy and traditional roles may not be absolutely exclusive, at some point they are likely to come into conflict.[4] The more individuals perceive their role as bringing "neutral competence" to the bureaucracy, the less inclined they will be to conceive of the job as representation or advocacy for one particular group.

Policy Outcomes Consistent with Minority Interests

Minority Representative Role

The next major question examined in the model is whether administrators who consider themselves representatives of minority interests will be able to see that those interests are reflected in policy outcomes. Administrators who embrace the minority representative role perception most strongly believe that they should act in favor of policies that address the needs of minority clients, support procedures that increase minority access to government programs, and work in other ways to help ensure that minority interests are not overlooked in policy decision making. As suggested in the literature on representative bureaucracy, this process is one means of providing that bureaucratic decisions reflect the diversity of attitudes, opinions, and perspectives in the population (Krislov and Rosenbloom 1981). The model in Figure 6.1 (page 115) proposes that to the degree that administrators hold these beliefs, specific policy outcomes under their control are more likely to be formulated in such a way as to ensure the protection of minority interests.

Traditional Bureaucratic Role

Adherence to the more traditional bureaucratic role perception should also have a direct effect on policy outcomes. Because this perception of the administrative role stresses the efficient implementation of agency programs and policies, administrators holding this view will be concerned primarily with objectivity and neutrality, rather than equity-based issues. When administrators operate from this perspective, it is likely that policy outcomes awarded to minority interests will be judged less important and, consequently, will be less likely to occur.

This study examines the process of active representation of minority interests (African Americans, Hispanics, and Native Americans) in the policy outputs of the Farmers Home Administration.[5] As in Chapter 5, the major dependent variable is loan eligibility decisions made by the agency in the Rural Housing Loans program. The analysis also examines the amount of publicity given to this program in the minority community.

Race and Ethnicity

Because the concept of the minority representative role introduced here recognizes that nonminority bureaucrats may also have been socialized to represent minority interests, the model includes a variable for race/ethnicity of the local administrator. The inclusion of this variable should indicate whether the adherence to the minority representative role exerts an influence on administrative behavior above and beyond race and ethnicity.

Operationalization of Model

Table 6.1 displays all variables used in the analysis (the Appendix describes the construction of the indexes in detail). In the first part of the model, the dependent variable is the extent to which FmHA county supervisors perceive their work role as a representative of minority interests. Eight questions were used to gauge the supervisor's attitude toward assuming this role (see the Appendix for the text of the items). In the second part of the model focusing on policy outcomes, the first dependent variable examined is the percentage of rural housing loan eligibility decisions in a county office awarded to minority applicants. Active representation might also be measured by the extent to which county supervisors target minorities when publicizing this program, and for that reason, outreach efforts designed to publicize the Rural Housing Loans program in minority communities are examined as well. Ordinary least squares regression is used to estimate each equation.

Table 6.1

Operationalization of Dependent and Independent Variables

Dependent Variables
　　Minority Representative Role Acceptance (Index 1 scaled 8 to 40)
　　Percentage of Eligibility Decisions Favoring Minorities (scaled 0 to 100 percent)
　　Extent to which County Supervisors Publicize Rural Housing Loans Program in
　　　　Minority Community (Index 3 scaled 0 to 9)

Independent Variables

Personal Factors
　Race/Ethnicity:
　　(0 = white)
　　(1 = minority)
　Education[a]
　　(1 = high school diploma)
　　(2 = some college)
　　(3 = bachelor's degree)
　　(4 = some graduate school)
　　(5 = master's degree)
　Type of Education
　　(0 = not educated at a traditionally all-black college or university)
　　(1 = educated at a traditionally all-black college or university)
　Age
　　(1995–Year of Birth)
　Party Identification
　　(1 = strong Democrat)
　　(2 = moderate Democrat)
　　(3 = independent)
　　(4 = moderate Republican)
　　(5 = strong Republican)

　　Because rural housing loan eligibility decisions will be awarded to minorities in part as a function of demand for such loans by minorities in a particular area, the equations examining this variable and the extent to which the program is publicized in the minority community introduce minority economic hardship and minority population in the area as control variables. The assumption is that minority hardship and population will serve as proxy measures for demand for FmHA loans from the minority community. By controlling for demand in this manner, the analysis will gauge more accurately the extent to which county supervisors engage in active representation in awarding loans and publicizing the program. Prior studies examining policy outputs have also used various combinations of area demographic characteristics as con-

Organizational Factors
   Number of Training Programs Attended in Past Year
   Years in Current Position
   Years of Federal Service
   Number of Minorities Working in County Office
Perceived Role Expectations
   Expected by Stakeholders to Work in Favor of the Delivery of Public Program
      Services in a Manner that Increases Minority Access (Index 4 scaled 0 to 8).
   Expected by Stakeholders to Implement Programs Consistent with Departmental
      Procedures (Index 5 scaled 0 to 8).
   Expected by Stakeholders to Implement Programs in a Manner that Increases
      Minority Access and to Implement Programs Consistent with Departmental
      Procedures (Index 6 scaled 0 to 8).
Role Perception
   Traditional Role Acceptance (Index 2 scaled 3 to 15)

Control Variables
   Minority Economic Hardship (Index 7 scaled 0 to 100). It is designed to control
   for expected "demand" or "share" of rural housing loans eligibility decisions
   favoring minorities.
   Minority Population. Percentage of population comprised of minorities in 1990.
   Political Representation (0, 1). Districts represented by a group member in the
   U.S. House of Representatives are coded 1.
   Political Ideology 1993 Americans for Democratic Action (ADA) rating for the
   FmHA district's House of Representatives member. The index is scaled from 0
   (conservative) to 100 (liberal).

   Notes:
   [a]No respondent indicated that she or he held a doctorate or law degree.
   [b]Stakeholders are district and state management, general public, minority community,
nonminority colleagues, minority colleagues, minority employee organizations,
professional associations, and local political officials.

---

trol variables (Meier and Stewart 1992; Meier 1993a; Hindera 1993a,
1993b). Similar to the analyses presented in Chapter 5, the model also
controls for the effects of minority political representation and political
ideology on resource allocations.

Examining the Linkages

Findings from the empirical analysis lend considerable support to the
linkages hypothesized in the model between demographic representation, the assumption of a minority representative role, and the realization of policy outputs consistent with minority group interests. Table
6.2 presents results from the regression analysis in which adherence to

the minority representative role perception by FmHA county supervisors is the dependent variable. Overall, the variables included in the model can account for 31 percent of the variation in minority representative role perceptions.

From the standpoint of representative bureaucracy, the most important finding in Table 6.2 is that minority status, as hypothesized, exerts a strong influence on adherence to the minority representative role. Minority FmHA supervisors are much more likely than nonminorities to perceive their role as a representative of minority interests. Crucial to the theory of representative bureaucracy, race and ethnicity appear to influence the attitudes and role perceptions of government employees regarding minority representation.

A number of other personal factors are also influential. For example, the level of formal education of the local supervisors apparently exerts a significant negative effect on acceptance of the minority representative role perception. As education level increases, respondents are less likely to see themselves as representatives of minority interests.[6] This finding contradicts the results of the early study by Meier and Nigro (1976) suggesting that administrators with more education will be more responsive to the needs of minorities, but it is consistent with Daley's (1984) later study of state government officials. The negative relationship between educational attainment and perceiving oneself as a minority representative may occur, in part, because education is related to personal ambition. Daley (1984) makes a similar argument after finding that administrators with more education are less supportive of efforts to achieve a representative bureaucracy. Furthermore, Henderson (1988) found that more educated public administrators are generally more ambitious. In the context of the FmHA, ambition may be driving both employee educational attainment and reluctance to actively represent minority interests. Given the recent history of the FmHA with respect to racial issues discussed above, it may well be that those who seek to advance in the organization, (i.e., those who are ambitious) will be hesitant to take on the minority representative role. If that is the case, then such a pattern of behavior would help to explain the negative association between education and acceptance of a minority representative role. Unfortunately, this study has no direct measure of administrators' ambition to allow a test of this hypothesis.

Other personal factors associated with the minority representative role perception are age and political party affiliation. Older administra-

Table 6.2

Regression Model for Minority Representative Role Perception

Independent Variables	Unstandardized Coefficient	Standard Error	Standardized Coefficient
Personal Factors			
Minority	4.47**	1.39	.32
Education level[1]	−1.01*	.51	−.13
Age	.20**	.08	.27
Party identification	−.96**	.43	−.16
Attended traditionally all-black university	1.20	1.48	.08
Organizational Factors			
Years in federal government	−.22**	.10	−.28
Number of days in training	−.01	.03	−.02
Years in position	.01	.07	.02
Presence of minority colleagues	−1.97	.88	−.16
Perceived Role Expectations			
Expected to increase minority access to programs	.83**	.28	.24
Expected to implement programs according to departmental practices and increase minority access	.87***	.26	.32
Expected to implement programs according to departmental practices	.26	.21	.13
Traditional Bureaucratic Role Perception	−.31*	.15	−.14

$$R^2 = .31$$
Adjusted R^2 .26
F = 5.85
Number of Cases = 184

[1]A two-tail signficance test is used for education since a directional relationship was not hypothesized for that variable. For all other variables included in the equation, a one-tail test is employed.
  *significant at .05
  **significant at .01
  ***significant at .001

tors are more likely to see their role as that of a minority representative, a finding compatible with the generational hypothesis offered earlier. Because older employees experienced the civil rights movement and the struggle of African Americans and other minorities to achieve legal and political representation and social equality, they may be more receptive to this role.[7] Also as hypothesized, acceptance of the minority representative role perception declines as allegiance to the Republican Party increases. Strong Republicans are much less likely to perceive their role as a representative of minority interests than are Democrats. This finding comports well with previous research on bureaucratic attitudes (Daley 1984; Thompson 1978).

With respect to the variables tapping organizational socialization, as expected, number of years in the federal service is negatively associated with assumption of the minority representative role. As tenure in the federal government increases (for those in the sample, this measure is effectively the same as years in the FmHA), administrators are less likely to adopt this role.[8] The other two measures of organizational socialization, days of training and years in the supervisor position, are not related significantly to the minority representative role.

Contrary to our expectation, the presence of minority co-workers in the FmHA local office is associated negatively with adherence to the minority representative role. The exact dynamic underlying that relationship is not clear. To clarify the relationship between working with minority co-workers and work role perceptions, future research must examine larger organizational units with more minority administrators in supervisory and nonsupervisory positions than the FmHA presents.[9]

The variables measuring the perceived role expectations of the FmHA county supervisors substantiate the relationships hypothesized by the model. To the degree that the supervisors believe that important actors in the policy environment (such as agency management, colleagues, employee organizations, the general public, the minority community, professional associations, and political officials) expect them to increase minority access or in other ways represent minority interests, they are much more likely to accept the minority representative role. In fact, even when county supervisors perceive that they are expected *both* to implement programs according to departmental practices *and* to increase minority access to programs and therefore seek a compromise between these two positions, they are still likely to adopt the minority representative role perception. By contrast, the belief on the part of these administrators that other actors expect them only to implement programs consistent with departmental procedures has no bearing on their assumption of a minority representative role.

Finally, the results in Table 6.2 confirm the hypothesized negative relationship between attachment to a traditional bureaucratic role perception and acceptance of the minority representative role. County supervisors who adhere to a more traditionally defined bureaucratic role where efficiency is the primary objective are not as likely to perceive their role as a representative of minority interests.

Tables 6.3 and 6.4 present results from the second part of the model examining the effect of the minority representative role perception on policy outputs consistent with minority interests. The findings strongly suggest that to the degree that the FmHA supervisors perceive their role as minority representatives, they will work to see that minority interests are reflected in the implementation of public programs. In Table 6.3, the dependent variable in the regression analysis is the percentage of loan eligibility determinations awarded to minorities by the local supervisor. Even when the demand for loans from the minority community is controlled statistically through the inclusion in the model of the minority hardship index, adherence to a minority representative role perception by local FmHA supervisors significantly increases the proportion of eligibility decisions favoring minorities. The result suggests that adherence to the minority representative role exerts an influence on administrative behavior above and beyond race and ethnicity. As anticipated, assumption of the traditional bureaucratic role perception is negatively associated with the percentage of eligibility decisions to minorities, although the coefficient does not attain statistical significance. The equation can account for 50 percent of the variation in loan determinations.

Table 6.4 presents the results of the regression analysis explaining the extent to which the FmHA county supervisors publicize the Rural Housing Loans program in the minority community. Analogous to the findings in Table 6.3, local supervisors who conceive their role as a representative of minority interests are more likely to publicize the loan program in this community. As before, assumption of the traditional bureaucratic role perception is negatively associated with the publicity effort, but here it is statistically significant. In other words, county supervisors who conceive of their role in a more traditional bureaucratic sense are less inclined to publicize the loan program in the minority community. The results of this model differ from the previous model in that minority status exerts a positive and statistically significant effect on publicizing the loan program. In this model, both race and adherence to the minority representative role have an influence on administrative behavior. Viewed collectively, Tables 6.3 and 6.4 provide substantial support for a linkage between the role perceptions of

Table 6.3

Regression Model for Percentage of Eligibility Determinations Awarded to Minorities

Independent Variables	Unstandardized Coefficient	Standard Error	Standardized Coefficient
Traditional bureaucratic role	−.37	0.51	−.04
Minority representative role	2.92***	0.25	.65
Minority	.79	3.64	.01
Minority hardship index	.60***	0.18	.17
Minority population	.00	0.00	.05
Minority House representative	2.73	3.61	.04
Political liberalism	−.07	0.07	−.05

$R^2 = .50$
Adjusted $R^2 =$
$F = 27.79$***
Number of Cases = 184

** significant at .05
** significant at .01
*** significant at .001

Table 6.4

Regression Model for Publicizing Rural Housing Loans Program in Minority Community

Independent Variables	Unstandardized Coefficient	Standard Error	Standardized Coefficient
Traditional role	−.08*	0.05	−.11
Minority representative role	.04*	0.02	.14
Minority	1.36***	0.34	.30
Minority hardship index	.03	0.02	.10
Minority population	.00	0.00	.08
Minority House representative	−.38	0.33	−.09
Political liberalism	.01	0.01	.05

$R^2 = .19$
Adjusted $R^2 = .16$
$F = 6.45$***
Number of Cases = 184

* significant at .05
** significant at .01
*** significant at .001

FmHA officials and their administrative behavior. Administrators who perceive their role as a representative of minority interests are more likely to engage in behaviors that benefit the minority community.

Conclusions

The findings of this study offer support for the concept of representative bureaucracy. Krislov (1974) once argued that examining passive representation was of limited usefulness. At best, the social origins of civil servants provide only indirect evidence of the representative character of the bureaucracy. Background reveals little about an individual's potential for representing the interests of people from similar backgrounds. In order to verify the assumptions of representative bureaucracy, scholars need to establish a relationship between demographic characteristics and work attitudes, and attitudes and administrative behaviors. This research has provided evidence for both of these linkages.

From the perspective of representative bureaucracy, the finding that race and ethnicity exert a strong influence on an administrator's view of his or her role is of critical importance. The relationship demonstrated here between minority status and acceptance of the minority representative role by local supervisors of the FmHA indicates that race and ethnicity make a significant difference in administrative perceptions. Socialization to the agency, or the public service more generally, does not overwhelm the importance of role perceptions or background characteristics in structuring bureaucratic attitudes. In turn, adherence to the minority representative role perception is positively associated with policy outcomes consistent with minority interests. When administrators see themselves as representatives of minority interests, policy outcomes responsive to those interests are more likely to be achieved.

Considered together, these results significantly reinforce the notion that the representativeness of a public agency can affect bureaucratic responsiveness to identifiable segments of the citizenry. The study thus substantiates research findings by Hindera (1993a, 1993b), Meier (1993a), and Meier and Stewart (1992) linking passive and active representation in other settings. This study also adds to our understanding of one mechanism by which active representation occurs: the administrative role perception.

Notes

A previous version of this chapter was presented at the Third National Public Management Research Conference, October 1995, in collaboration with Jeff Brudney and J. Edward Kellough.

1. Supervisors in the following states were surveyed: Alabama, Arkansas, Georgia, Kentucky, Louisiana, Mississippi, North Carolina, South Carolina, Tennessee, and Texas. Responses were received from 234 individuals, or 61 percent of the sample. Of this group, 184 had complete data on the items included in the analysis.

2. Meier and Nigro (1976) included the following demographic variables in their analysis: father's social class, urbanism, region, education, age, respondent's first occupation, race, and sex. Moreover, they examined the following 12 policy areas: environment, space, health care, urban problems, crime control, drug abuse, education, defense, foreign aid, welfare, minorities, and agriculture. Of these 12 policy areas, organizational socialization was more important than demographic factors in 10 areas. In one case, welfare, the influences of social origins and organizational socialization were the same. On the issue of improving the conditions of minorities, demographic factors (including race) were more important than organizational socialization.

3. Meier (1993a) found that the relationship between the presence of minority administrators in an organization and organizational outcomes favoring minority interests is nonlinear. More specifically, Meier found that when only a few minority administrators are present in an organization, policy outputs favoring minority interests decline, but when minority representation becomes larger, and as it continues to increase after that point, policy outputs favoring minority interests increase. Meier suggests that the relationship is negative when only a small number of minority administrators is present because, being only a few, those administrators are less likely to get support from their nonminority co-workers. In that situation, minority administrators may well adhere to the minority representative role perception, but organizational outputs do not serve the interests of the minority community. In effect, there are too few administrators adhering to the representative role.

At this point, the model is oriented toward identifying factors that may lead an administrator to adopt the minority representative role. It is reasonable to expect that an administrator will be more likely to adopt that role when minority co-workers are present. The question of how adherence to that role ultimately impacts agency outputs is examined in the second part of the model.

4. The factors explaining a minority advocacy role perception are drawn from the representative bureaucracy and minority administrators literature. This model is not designed to explain the determinants of a traditional role perception, and an analysis of a traditional role perception using this model would be limited due to specification error. An examination of the regression results for a traditional role perception supports this supposition. The personal, organizational, and environmental variables explained less than 5 percent of the variance in traditional role

perception. Future research should develop a model to explain conditions under which individuals assume a traditional bureaucratic role.

5. Of the sample of respondents, 18.4 percent were African Americans, 2.7 percent were Hispanic, 1.8 percent were Native Americans, 76.7 percent were white, and 0.4 percent identified themselves as "other."

6. The possibility that education may have an impact on minorities different from its impact on nonminorities was tested by examining the effects of a variable interacting education with minority status. The interaction proved to be insignificant.

7. Substituting a "civil rights generation" dummy variable into the model in place of the age variable produced results that were nearly identical to those obtained with the age variable, although the R^2 value fell from .31 to .29.

8. I spoke to officials in twenty-three FmHA state offices and the Washington, D.C., office regarding the relationship between time in the agency and time in the federal government. FmHA officials indicated that almost all county supervisors advance through the ranks of the FmHA and have spent most of their federal government careers in the agency.

9. County offices are small, averaging about three employees. Minority co-workers in these offices tend to be clerical employees, who may have little effect on the work attitudes and role perceptions of the county supervisor, their hierarchical superior.

7

Conclusions

In his 1997 State of the Union address, President Clinton proclaimed that as a nation, diversity "is our greatest strength." Continuing, he acknowledged that intolerance and prejudice still exist in our society, citing the recent rash of African-American church fires and the bombing of the Oklahoma City Federal Building. Other events, such as the L.A. riots triggered by the Rodney King verdict and the controversies provoked by the O.J. Simpson trial, have deeply divided the public opinion along race lines. Given the considerable distance between African Americans' and Caucasians' understandings of these issues, the relevance of demographic characteristics in offering information and perspective becomes apparent. Such attitudinal divides heighten society's awareness that individuals hear, interpret, and process information through their own filters, life experiences, and frames of reference. Therefore, it is difficult, if not impossible, for an individual to comprehend completely how another person, from a different walk of life, could process and react to an incident in such a markedly different way.

Diversity, by definition, implies differences. With a nation comprised of citizens from such a wide scope of backgrounds, perspectives, and experiences, how do we create a community and a political environment that values and promotes uniqueness and diversity in its practices? One obvious means is through dialogue and actions of political actors, and another, as evidenced by this research, is through bureaucratic institutions. Minority public officials afford substantive representation of minority concerns. Thus, denying employment to certain groups will not only serve to alter their opportunities, it will change the policy dialogue, and will likely limit group access to political resources allocated by bureaucratic agencies.

Representativeness and Representing:
What We Have Learned

Hanna Pitkin (1967) argued in her incisive book, *The Concept of Representation*, that it is essential to distinguish between representativeness and representing. Representativeness is similar to passive representation, that is, it focuses on the characteristics of representatives. Representing, on the other hand, most closely reflects active representation. It concerns the choice of representatives to act or make decisions that reflect opinions and desires of those they represent. Although directly related, the two terms are not synonymous in definition and in practice.

Representativeness in the FmHA

This study demonstrates that equal employment opportunity is still not a reality in the Farmers Home Administration for African Americans, Hispanics, Asian Americans, and women. Although minorities and women have made progress in the FmHA, they still hold fewer key decision-making positions and many tend to be saturated in lower-level positions. Whether underrepresentation of these groups is intentional or institutional is not examined in this present endeavor. At a minimum, however, the history of the FmHA suggests an institutional pattern that continues to perpetuate itself.

Given the number and geographic dispersion of FmHA field offices, this research was able to examine employment patterns of minorities and women across FmHA districts. African-American representation in FmHA districts is affected by African-American resources (population and education), organizational structure and climate, and region. Specifically, African Americans are able to gain a larger share of FmHA district positions when African Americans work in the state office. In addition, southern and midwestern FmHA districts employ significantly more African Americans than FmHA districts located in other parts of the country.

As with African Americans, employment of Hispanics in FmHA districts is a function of Hispanic resources (Hispanic population), region, and organizational climate, as well as the political environment. FmHA districts in the south, midwest, and west regions employ more Hispanics than offices located in the northeast. The employment levels of Hispanics were inversely related to the employment levels of African Americans, suggesting that Hispanics compete with African Americans for FmHA jobs. Hispanic access to jobs is affected by both Hispanic representation in Congress and political liberalism. As would be expected, the presence of a Hispanic congress person results in larger percentages of Hispanic FmHA employees.

Asian-American access to FmHA district jobs depends on Asian-American resources (population) and organizational factors. The single most important determinant of Asian-American employment is the proportion of Asian Americans living in the FmHA district. As the Asian population increases, Asian Americans have secured a significantly larger share of FmHA positions. In addition, Asian Americans fared better working in environments with Asian Americans represented in the state office.

Research reveals that Native American representation in FmHA districts is a determinant of Native American population size, Native American representation in state offices, African-American FmHA district employment, and funding. FmHA districts serving more Native American constituents tend to employ more Native American personnel. As with other groups, Native Americans attain more positions when Native Americans are represented in the state office. As expected, the success of African Americans had a negative effect on the employment opportunities of Native Americans.

Female employment in FmHA districts is affected by organizational culture, region, and political representation. In particular, southern and midwestern FmHA districts had a larger share of women on staff than other areas. Female access to FmHA positions is a function of female representation in both the state office and Congress. In addition, women secured fewer positions in FmHA districts that employed African Americans.

In order to promote representation of groups, it is critical to understand factors that facilitate group representation. This research reveals that employment patterns are driven by a group's resources, region, intergroup competition, and representation of a group in high-level positions within the bureaucracy and in Congress. Understanding these factors will help in designing policies that promote diversity.

Descriptive or passive representation is a powerful symbol that communicates a message about representing. The lack of representation of minorities and women in key decision-making positions has become associated with a sense of failure on the part of bureaucratic institutions to represent the substantive interests of the minorities and women. Gregory Thielemann and Joseph Stewart's perceptive article, "A Demand-Side Perspective on the Importance of Representative Bureaucracy: AIDS, Ethnicity, Gender, and Sexual Orientation" (1996), provides a new perspective about how citizens, particularly clients, benefit from a representative bureaucracy. They found that "if clients of HIV service delivery agencies care about the characteristics of those who run and staff the service delivery bureaucracy, and consequently are more or less likely to use the services depending on its representativeness, they exhibit a demand for a representative bureaucracy" (Thielemann and Stewart 1996, 169). Although this research does not examine demand for FmHA representation, it does demonstrate that a representative bureaucracy produces tangible benefits to groups represented.

Representing in the FmHA

The findings suggest that program resource allocation is affected by the staffing of the service delivery unit. This study provides substantial evidence that districts with higher percentages of African-American, Hispanic, and Asian-American supervisors awarded more FmHA Rural Housing Loans determinations to African-American, Hispanic, and Asian-American citizens, respectively. The results of this research are especially significant because representatives are found representing their constituents in an organizational culture whose primary mission does not emphasize minority issues and that has implemented policies historically that have adversely affected minorities.

In a more thorough investigation into the dynamics of representing, this research revealed some interesting and complex findings about the development of administrative roles and their subsequent impact on administrative behaviors. Race/ethnicity is a critical factor in predicting whether an individual perceived his or her role as an advocate or representative of minority interests. The traditional measures of organizational socialization, such as years of federal service, years in position, and training, do not overwhelm the effects of racial/ethnic background. In fact, only years of federal service was significant in this model. This is a particularly important finding as some earlier research indicated that agency socialization tended to overcome the influences of demographic background characteristics (Meier and

Nigro 1976). Although the relationship between age and minority advocacy or representative role perception is statistically significant, the direction of the relationship does not support an "organizational socialization" argument. Instead, it suggests that older employees are more likely to perceive a minority advocate role. As mentioned earlier, this may be due in part to the effects of age cohorts. For example, older administrators are likely to have experienced and participated in the civil rights movement.

The results provide considerable support for the hypothesized relationship between political ideology and assuming a minority advocacy role. Administrators who identified themselves as liberals are much more inclined to take on a minority advocacy or representative role. Also, individuals who perceived that internal or external actors in the policy process expected them to increase minority access to programs are more inclined to assume a role representing minority concerns. Thus, environmental conditions can sharpen an employee's perception of his or her work role and encourage him or her to assume certain responsibilities. Furthermore, individuals who view their role more traditionally are not as likely to perceive their role as that of an advocate or representative of minority interests.

The relationship between presence of minority colleagues in county offices and a minority advocacy role perception is perplexing. The evidence suggests that administrators who work with minorities are less likely to assume a minority advocacy role. Several possible explanations were offered in Chapter 6. However, to better understand this relationship, case studies of FmHA county offices employing different percentages of minorities are needed.

The findings also lend support for the relationship between role perceptions and policy outputs. The evidence suggests that administrators who perceive their role as that of an advocate or representative of minority interests are more likely to make decisions that benefit the minority community. That is, individuals who perceive their role as minority advocates award a larger share of loan eligibility decisions to minorities and are more likely to publicize the Rural Housing Loans program in the minority community.

Overall, the results yielded support for the major theoretical linkages suggested in the representative bureaucracy literature: demographic backgrounds and socialization experiences significantly influence attitudes/role perceptions, and attitudes/role perceptions are significantly related to administrative decisions and actions. The determinacy of the relationship between personal characteristics and attitudes/values, and subsequently the relationship between attitudes/values and decisions, is one of the most powerful arguments in support of establishing a system to provide representation of such characteristics.

Policy Implications

These findings confirm that increasing the number of minority employees makes a real difference in how resources are allocated. The research on determinants of passive representation suggest several policy alternatives that have been shown to increase minority and gender representation. In all but one case, minorities and women held a larger share of positions when they were represented in the state director's office. Thus, one means of ensuring greater representation is to advance women and minorities into management positions within the state director's office. Increasing representation in the state office, however, is not merely a bureaucratic decision, it is a political exercise. FmHA state directors are political appointees who are then largely responsible for making employment decisions within the state director's office. Moreover, in the case of Hispanics and women, employment patterns were influenced significantly by political representation in Congress. Given these two indicators, it appears that FmHA employment is in part politically influenced.

This research also cautions practitioners to be sensitive to inter-minority group competition when designing personnel policies. Considerable evidence was found that African Americans tended to succeed in employment opportunities at the expense of other underrepresented groups. It may be necessary to design recruiting strategies to specifically target all minority groups, especially those with the education and skills to hold decision-making positions. Agencies might recruit from educational institutions and other employment entities in the area. It is possible, however, that agencies will encounter competition from other agencies and private businesses for the top minority and female job candidates.

The elimination of affirmative action policies could ultimately reduce the percentage of racial and ethnic minorities employed by public bureaucracies. If colleges and universities abandon affirmative action programs, the percentage of minorities graduating with college degrees may fall. As a result, agencies would have a more difficult time recruiting minority candidates, and therefore minority agency employment would decline. Subsequently, declining entry-level minority employment will lead to fewer minorities in a position to advance into key agency decision-making positions. Moreover, if agencies abandon affirmative action policies, they might place a lower priority on recruiting, hiring, and promoting minorities and women. In some cases, such as the FmHA, increasing minority representation has proven to be a tangible means of addressing historic program inequities and biases; unfortunately, however, reducing minority representation could hinder future progress.

The results of this study suggest that an effective means of ensuring that minority interests are represented in administrative decision-making processes is to employ minority administrators. However, only to the degree that other actors in the policy process, such as colleagues, elected officials, and the community, value and support a minority advocacy or representative role, are individuals more likely to assume this role. Thus, an agency must work to create a culture that values and encourages diversity and representation in its policies and practices.

Future Directions in Representative Bureaucracy

In addition to the implications discussed above, several questions are worth raising. One fundamental issue that may warrant attention is whether active representation is always good since it may conflict with notions of bureaucratic neutrality. Based on the findings of this research, employing minority administrators helps to ensure that minority interests and concerns are taken into consideration. The extent to which one supports the goal of incorporating minority needs and concerns in policies will dictate the extent to which one perceives active representation as beneficial. To exclude minorities from participating in public organizations is clearly an injustice. It is likely that a bureaucracy that employs all white administrators will yield different decisions and policies than a bureaucracy that employs a diverse work force. Having a work force that reflects the demographic characteristics of society will help ensure that the bureaucracy is responsive to the needs and interests of all groups and hence provides a means of controlling the exercise of bureaucratic power in the policy process. The question then becomes, how integrated should public organizations be?

Should all agencies be integrated proportionate to the racial, ethnic, and gender composition of society? One possible answer is that agencies should be integrated to the fullest extent possible given the labor pool from which they recruit employees. An integrated work force helps to ensure that the values and interests of all groups in society are articulated and hence brought to bear upon decisions made and policies formulated. As a result, the agency will be more responsive to the needs and concerns of the groups represented.

Given the culture and history of the FmHA, the findings of this research should hold for other service agencies; that is, organizations that have as their primary goal promoting the welfare of their clients (Hill 1976). However, future research should replicate this study in other organizational settings. One possibility is to test these relationships in an agency with larger field offices in order to flesh out the relationship between minority colleagues and minority advocacy role expectations. In addition, future studies of active representation should consider supplementing survey data with personal interviews and observations of the minority and nonminority administrators. This approach would provide additional insight and information about organizational context, and could reveal differences and similarities between minority and nonminority administrators. For example, do minority and nonminority administrators treat minority and nonminority clients differently or interact differently with them?

As discussed in Chapter 5, the insignificant findings for women raise a number of questions. What perspectives and goals of women are represented by female administrators? What actually happens as women gain a greater share of decision-making authority? Will increasing female representation make a difference in decision-making and policy outputs? Future research should focus on these issues and seek to identify under what conditions and for what types of policies female administrators engage in behavior that actively represents the interests of women.

Finally, given the paucity of research on role perceptions of administrators, further study of how administrators view their work roles and responsibilities is warranted. Attention should be given to the tradeoffs between different values, such as responsiveness to minority interests, efficiency, public participation, and the impact of contradictory role perceptions on administrative actions.

Native Americans are the only overrepresented minority group in this study, and they are the only group in which passive and active representation are not linked significantly. This study's findings indicate that for this particular program Native American administrators do not award a larger share of resources statistically to Native Americans than other administrators. The insignificant findings for Native Americans also raise a number of questions. What actually happens as Native Americans gain a greater share of decision-making authority? Will increasing Native American representation make a difference in decision making and policy outputs in other organizational settings? Future research should focus specifically on Native American administrators and seek to identify under what conditions and for what types of policies Native American administrators engage in behavior that actively represents the interests of Native Americans. Moreover, future studies should concentrate on understanding Native American culture and its relationship to administrative roles and leadership.

Another possible avenue for future research is to investigate in more detail subgroups within racial and ethnic communities. An underlying assumption of research linking passive and active representation is that racial and ethnic minorities respond to a broader sense of representation within their groups. For example, this study assumes that Native Americans represent the interests of Native American citizens regardless of their tribal identity. Research needs to explicitly focus on intraminority group differences. That is, to what extent do agency employees from minority subgroups represent citizens from other subgroups within a minority community? For example, do Cherokee civil servants actively represent the interests of Comanche tribal members?

Attempts should be made to bridge studies of demand for representative bureaucracy to the process of active representation. Thielemann and Stewart (1996, 172) suggest that "developing more understanding of the demand for representative bureaucracy and the conditions under which it exists should be high on the agenda of public administration researchers." Moreover, research should also explore whether the demand for representative bureaucracy drives employment levels and subsequent bureaucratic behavior. A better understanding of the dynamics between the representatives and those represented would provide considerable insight into the process of representation.

Appendix:
Construction of Indexes

Index 1: Minority Representative Role Acceptance

The following questions were incorporated in the representative of minority interests index.

To what extent do you agree or disagree with the following statements?
(1 [disagree] to 5 [agree]):

I should seek to provide information to policy makers to assist them in making decisions concerning minority community needs and perspectives.

I should recommend or actively advocate in favor of policies which address the needs and concerns of minority clients.

I should be supportive of procedures which may result in greater and more equitable access by minorities to federal programs and services.

I should actively advocate in favor of a more equitable distribution of program services to minorities including recommending procedural service delivery alternatives when necessary.

I should be supportive of or encourage Federal and/or departmental change when necessary to insure the representation of minorities in governmental affairs.

I should recommend and/or actively advocate in favor of institutional changes which may result in a greater governmental responsiveness to minorities.

I should specifically encourage and recruit qualified minorities for professional and administrative federal employment.

I should actively advocate in favor of hiring and promotional practices which may result in greater minority representation and ethnic balance in federal personnel.

The questions were summed to create an index from 8 to 40. A score of 8 indicates that an individual does not perceive his or her role as that of an advocate or representative of minority interest, while a score of 40 suggests that an individual strongly perceives his or her role as that of an active representative.

Index 2: Traditional Role Acceptance

The following questions were incorporated in the traditional role index.

To what extent do you agree or disagree with the following statements?
(1 [disagree] to 5 [agree]):

Regarding program implementation, I should limit my concern to the efficient carrying out of my own departmental programs and duties.

I should limit my concern with "how" federal programs and services are implemented, and in particular to the efficient execution of my own departmental duties.

I should actively advocate in favor of hiring and promotion of individuals with a focus on equal opportunity and merit.

The questions were summed to create an index from 3 to 15. A score of 3 indicates that an individual does not perceive his or her role in terms of efficient execution of duties, while a score of 15 suggests that an individual strongly perceives his or her role in terms of efficiently implementing responsibilities.

**Index 3: Extent to Which County Supervisors Publicize
Rural Housing Loans Program in Minority Community**

The following questions were combined to gauge the extent to which a county supervisor publicizes the Rural Housing Loans program in the minority community.

How often do you use the following ways to publicize the Rural Housing Loans Program? (1 [never] to 4 [very often]):
Churches
Minority Outreach Programs
Minority Community Organizations

The questions were summed and 3 subtracted to create an index from 0 to 9. A score of 0 indicates that an individual never publicizes the program in these places, while a score of 9 suggests that an individual very often targets the minority community to publicize the Rural Housing Loans program.

Indexes 4 to 6: Role Expectations

We asked county supervisors about their perceptions of the role expectations that the following groups held for them: district and state management, general public, minority community, nonminority community, minority colleagues, minority employee organizations, professional associations, and local political officials. **For each group, the respondent could choose** *one* **of the four responses.**

Expect me to advocate in favor of the delivery of programs and services in a manner which may increase minority access.

Expect me to implement programs and services consistent with established departmental procedures and past practices.

Expect me to both continue existing program and service delivery practices and to seek procedures for increasing access for minorities.

Hold no expectation either way regarding my involvement in program implementation and service delivery.

We created three indexes from this group of questions. Respondents assessed their perceptions about the role expectations of the eight groups listed above, and for each group, the individual selected only one of the four responses. For the first three responses, the number of times an individual selected each response was counted. For example, an individual may have perceived that five of the eight groups expected him or her to advocate in favor of delivery of programs and services in a manner that increases minority access. If so, on index 4, the individual would receive a score of 5.

Index 7: Minority Economic Hardship

Due to the high intercorrelations of area characteristics that may affect the demand for rural housing loans, such as unemployment, income level, and poverty, this study used an index developed by the Brookings Institution to gauge area hardship. Six measures available from the 1990 census comprise the hardship index:

Poverty: Percentage of minorities living in poverty
Area population: Percentage of population comprised of members of minority groups
Unemployment: Percentage of minority labor force that is unemployed
Dependency: Percentage of selected minority population that is less than 18 or over 64 years of age
Education: Percentage of minority population twenty-five years of age or more with less than a twelfth-grade education
Income Level: Per capita income of minorities

Each of these ratios was standardized to give equal weight to each of these comparative measures (see Nathan and Adams 1976, 1989; O'Sullivan and Rassel 1995). The following formula was applied to each of the hardship indicators to standardize them:

$$x = \left(\frac{Y-Y\text{min}}{Y\text{max}-Y\text{min}} \right) 100$$

where: X = standardized ratio to be created
Y = variable calculated from census data
Y_{max} = maximum value of Y
Y_{min} = minimum value of Y

The standardized values indicate where each area served by a county office is on a continuum of hardship ranging from the "worst" area to the "best" area. Accordingly, the ratio for each hardship indicator ranges from a value of 0 (the area with the lowest rating) to 100 (the area with the highest rating).

The standardized indicators were summed and then divided by six. The values of the hardship index can range from 0 to 100. The higher the minorities' hardship index score, the more adverse the minorities' economic situation is in an area.

Bibliography

Aberbach, Joel D., and Bert A. Rockman, 1988. "Mandates or Mandarins? Control and Discretion in the Modern Administrative State." *Public Administration Review*, vol. 48 (March/April), pp. 606–612.

Agricultural Credit 28 *U.S.C.* §1921 (1958).

Ahrentzen, Sherry, 1985. "Residential Fit and Mobility among Low-Income, Female-Headed Family Households in the United States." In *Housing Needs and Policy Approaches: Trends in Thirteen Countries,* edited by Willem van Vliet, Elizabeth Huttman, and Sylvia Fava. Durham, NC: Duke University Press.

Americans for Democratic Action, 1993. "1993 Voting Record." *ADA Today*, vol. 49 (March), pp. 1–11.

Babbie, Earl, 1983. *The Practice of Social* Research. 3rd edition. Belmont, CA: Wadsworth.

Baldwin, Sidney, 1968. *Poverty and Politics*. Chapel Hill, NC: University of North Carolina Press.

Barke, Richard, and William Riker, 1982. "A Political Theory of Regulation with Some Observations on Railway Abandonments." *Public Choice*, vol. 39, pp. 73–106.

Bayes, Jane, 1989. "Women in California Executive Branch of Government." In *Gender, Bureaucracy, and Democracy*, edited by Mary M. Hale and Rita Mae Kelly. Westport, CT: Greenwood Press.

Bean, Frank D., and Marta Tienda, 1987. *The Hispanic Population of the United States*. New York: Russell Sage Foundation.

Berry, William D., and Stanley Feldman, 1985. *Multiple Regression in Practice*. Newbury Park, CA: Sage Publications.

Bianchi, Suzanne M., Reynolds Farley, and Daphne Spain, 1986. "Racial Inequalities in Housing: An Examination of Recent Trends." In *Race, Ethnicity, and Minority Housing in the United States*, edited by Jamshid A. Momeni. Westport, CT: Greenwood Press.

Birch, Eugenie, ed., 1985. *The Unsheltered Woman: Women and Housing in the 80's*. New Brunswick, NJ: Rutgers University Press.

———, 1989. "Women and Shelter: Needs and Issues." *In Housing Issues of the 1990s*, edited by Sara Rosenberry and Chester Hartman. New York: Praeger.

Bozeman, Barry, 1993. *Public Management: The State of the Art. San Francisco*, CA: Jossey-Bass.

Brewer, Gene A., 1995. "Incidence of Whistleblowing in the Public and Private Sectors." Unpublished manuscript.

Brown, Jonathan, 1992. "Opening the Book on Lending Discrimination." *Multinational Monitor*, vol. 13 (November), pp. 8–14.

Buchanan, James M., 1972. "Toward Analysis of Closed Behavioral Systems." In *Theory of Public Choice: Political Applications of Economics*, edited by James M. Buchanan and Robert D. Tollison. Ann Arbor: University of Michigan Press.

Bryner, Gary C., 1987. *Bureaucratic Discretion: Law and Policy in Federal Regulatory Agencies*. New York: Pergamon Press.

Calvert, Randall, Mathew McCubbins, and Barry Weingast, 1989. "A Theory of Political Control of Agency Discretion." *American Journal of Political Science*, vol. 33, pp. 588–610.

———, 1988. "Congressional Influence over Policymaking: The Case of the FTC." In *Congress: Structure and Policy*, edited by Mathew McCubbins and Terry Sullivan. Cambridge: Cambridge University Press.

Canner, Glenn B., Wayne Passmore, and Dolores Smith, 1994. "Residential Lending to Low-Income and Minority Females: Evidence from the 1992 HMDA Data." *Federal Reserve Bulletin*, vol. 80 (February), pp. 79–108.

Cary, William L., 1967. *Politics and the Regulatory Agencies*. New York: McGraw-Hill.

Cayer, N. Joseph, and Lee Sigelman, 1980. "Minorities and Women in State and Local Government: 1973–1975." *Public Administration Review*, vol. 40 (September/October), pp. 443–450.

Chubb, John E., 1985. "The Political Economy of Federalism." *The American Political Science Review*, vol. 79 (December), pp. 994–1015.

Conway, M. Margaret, David W. Ahern, and Gertrude A. Steuernagel, 1995. *Women and Public Policy: A Revolution in Progress*. Washington, D.C.: Congressional Quarterly.

Cook, Brian J., 1992. "The Representative Function of Bureaucracy: Public Administration in Constitutive Perspective." *Administration and Society*, vol. 23 (February), pp. 403–429.

Cornwell, Christopher, and J. Edward Kellough, 1994. "Women and Minorities in Federal Government Agencies: Examining Evidence from Panel Data." *Public Administration Review*, vol. 54 (May/June), pp. 265–270.

Dahl, Robert, 1947. "The Science of Public Administration: Three Problems." *Public Administration Review*, vol. 7 (January/February), pp. 1–11.

Daley, Dennis, 1984. "Political and Occupational Barriers to the Implementation of Affirmative Action: Administrative, Executive, and Legislative Attitudes Toward Representative Bureaucracy." *Review of Public Personnel Administration*, vol. 4 (Summer), pp. 4–15.

Darden, Joe T., 1986. "Accessibility to Housing: Differential Residential Segregation for Blacks, Hispanics, American Indians, and Asians." In *Race, Ethnicity, and Minority Housing in the United States*, edited by Jamshid A. Momeni. Westport, CT: Greenwood Press.

Davidson, Osha, 1987. "Farms Without Farmers." *The Progressive*, vol. 51 (August), pp. 25–27.

Davis, Charles, and Jonathan West, 1985. "Implementing Public Programs: Equal Opportunity, Affirmative Action, and Administrative Policy Options." *Review of Public Personnel Administration*, vol. 4 (Summer), pp. 16–30.

Davis, Kenneth C., 1969. *Discretionary Justice: A Preliminary Inquiry*. Baton Rouge: Louisiana State University Press.

Denhardt, Robert, and Linda deLeon, 1995. "Great Thinkers in Personnel Management." In *Handbook of Public Personnel Administration*, edited by Jack Rabin. New York: Marcel Dekken.

Dimock, Marshall, 1980. *Law and Dynamic Administration*. New York: Praeger.

Dodd, Lawrence, and Richard Schott, 1979. *Congress and the Administrative State*. New York: Free Press.

Doig, Jameson W., and Erwin C. Hargrove, 1987. " 'Leadership' and Political Analysis." In *Leadership and Innovation: A Biographic Perspective on Entrepreneurs in Government*, edited by Jameson W. Doig and Erwin C. Hargrove. Baltimore, MD: The Johns Hopkins University Press.

Dometrius, Nelson C., 1984. "Minorities and Women among State Agency Leaders." *Social Science Quarterly*, vol. 65 (March), pp. 127–137.

Dometrius, Nelson C., and Lee Sigelman, 1984. "Assessing Progress Toward Affirmative Action Goals in State and Local Governments: A New Benchmark." *Public Administration Review*, vol. 44 (May/June), pp. 241–246.

Downs, Anthony, 1967. *Inside Bureaucracy*. Boston: Little, Brown.

Duerst-Lahti, Georgia, and Cathy Marie Johnson, 1992. "Management Styles, Stereotypes, and Advantages." In *Women and Men of the States: Public Administrators at the State Level*, edited by Mary E. Guy. Armonk, NY: M.E. Sharpe.

Duke, Lois Lovelace, 1992. "Career Development and Affirmative Action." In *Women and Men of the States: Public Administrators at the State Level*, edited by Mary E. Guy. Armonk, NY: M.E. Sharpe.

Duncan Phil, ed., 1994. *Congressional Quarterly's Politics in America 1994: The 103rd Congress*. Washington, D.C.: CQ Press.

Dye, Thomas, and James Renick, 1981. "Political Power and City Jobs: Determinants of Minority Employment." *Social Science Quarterly*, vol. 62 (September), pp. 475–486.

Eisinger, Peter, K., 1982. "Black Employment in Municipal Jobs: The Impact of Black Political Power." *American Political Science Review*, vol. 76 (June), pp. 380–392.

Eribes, Richard A., N. Joseph Cayer, Albert K. Karnig, and Susan Welch, 1989. "Women in Municipal Bureaucracies of the Southwest." In *Gender, Bureaucracy, and Democracy*, edited by Mary M. Hale and Rita Mae Kelly. Westport, CT: Greenwood Press.

Fesler, James W., 1975. "Public Administration and the Social Sciences: 1946 to 1960." In *Past, Present, and Future*, edited by Dwight Waldo. University: The University of Alabama Press.

Finer, Herman, 1941. "Administrative Responsibility in Democratic Government." *Public Administration Review*, vol. 1 (Summer), pp. 335–350.

Frederickson, H. George, 1971. "Toward a New Public Administration." In *Toward a New Public Administration: The Minnowbrook Perspective*, edited by Frank Marini. Scranton, PA: Chandler.

————, 1976. "The Lineage of New Public Administration." *Administration and Society*, vol. 8 (August), pp. 149–174.

————, ed., 1993. *Ethics and Public Administration*. Armonk, NY: M.E. Sharpe.

French, John R.P., Jr., and Bertram Raven, 1959. "The Bases of Social Power." In *Studies and Social Power*, edited by Dorwin Wright. Ann Arbor, MI: Institute for Social Research, University of Michigan.

Friedrich, Carl, 1940. "Public Policy and the Nature of Administrative Responsibility." In *Public Policy*, edited by C. J. Friedrich and E. S. Mason. Cambridge, MA: Harvard University Press.

Gallas, Nesta M., 1985. "Representativeness: A New Merit Principle." *Public Personnel Management*, vol. 14 (Spring), pp. 25–31.

Garand, James C., Catherine T. Parkhurst, and Rusanne Jourdan Seoud, 1991. "Bureaucrats, Policy Attitudes, and Political Behavior: Extension of the Bureau Voting Model of Government Growth." *Journal of Public Administration Research and Theory*, vol. 1 (April), pp. 177–212.

Garham, David, 1975. "Foreign Service Elitism and U.S. Foreign Affairs." *Public Administration Review*, vol. 35 (January/February), pp. 44–51.

Gelb, Joyce, and Marian Lief Palley, 1982. *Women and Public Policies*. New Brunswick, NJ: Princeton University Press.

Gibson, Frank K., and Samuel Yeager, 1975. "Trends in the Federal Employment of Blacks." *Public-Personnel Management*, vol. 4 (May/June), pp. 189–195.

Gilbert, Charles E., 1959. "The Framework of Administrative Responsibility." *The Journal of Politics*, vol. 21 (August), pp. 373–407.

Goggin, Malcolm, Ann O'M Bowman, James P. Lester, and Laurence J. O'Toole, Jr., 1990. *Implementation Theory and Practice: Toward a Third Generation*. New York: HarperCollins.

Golembiewski, Robert T., 1969. "Organizational Development in Public Agencies." *Public Administration Review*, vol. 29 (July/August), pp. 367–377.

Good, Paul, 1968. *Cycle to Nowhere*. Washington, D.C.: GPO.

Goodnow, Frank, 1900. *Politics and Administration*. New York: Macmillan.

Goodsell, Charles T., 1985. *The Case for Bureaucracy: A Public Administration Polemic*. 2nd edition. Chatham, NJ: Chatham House.

Grabosky, Peter N., and David H. Rosenbloom, 1975. "Racial and Ethnic Integration in the Federal Service." *Social Science Quarterly*, vol. 56 (June), pp. 71–84.

Grady, Dennis O., 1989. "Economic Development and Administrative Power Theory: A Comparative Analysis of State Development Agencies." *Policy Studies Review*, vol. 8 (Winter), pp. 322–339.

Gruber, Judith E., 1987. *Controlling Bureaucracies: Dilemmas in Democratic Governance*. Berkeley: University of California Press.

Gugliotta, Guy, 1994. "10 Agencies Launch Effort to Curb Loan Bias: Cisneros, Reno Lead Coordinated Strategy." *The Washington Post*, 9 March, p. 1(D).

Guinier, Lani, 1994. *The Tyranny of the Majority: Fundamental Fairness in Representative Democracy*. New York: Free Press.

Gulick, Luther, and Lydall Urwick, 1937. *Papers on the Science of Public Administration*. New York: Institute of Public Administration.

Guy, Mary E., 1992. "Summing Up What We Know." In *Women and Men of the States: Public Administrators at the State Level*, edited by Mary E. Guy. Armonk, NY: M.E. Sharpe.

Guy, Mary E., and Georgia Duerst-Lahti, 1992. "Agency Culture and Its Effect on Managers." In *Women and Men of the States: Public Administrators at the State Level*, edited by Mary E. Guy. Armonk, NY: M.E. Sharpe.

Guy, Mary E., and Lois Lovelace Duke, 1992. "Personal and Social Background as Determinants of Position." In *Women and Men of the States: Public Administrators at the State Level*, edited by Mary E. Guy. Armonk, NY: M.E. Sharpe.

Hadwiger, Don F., 1973. "Experience of Black Farmers Home Administration Local Office Chiefs." *Public Personnel Management*, vol. 2 (January/February), pp. 49–54.

Hale, Mary M., 1992. "Mentoring." In *Women and Men of the States: Public Administrators at the State Level*, edited by Mary E. Guy. Armonk, NY: M.E. Sharpe.

Hale, Mary M., and M. Frances Branch, 1992. "Policy Preferences on Workplace Reform." In *Women and Men of the States: Public Administrators at the State Level*, edited by Mary E. Guy. Armonk, NY: M.E. Sharpe.

Hale, Mary M., and Rita Mae Kelly, 1989a. "Gender, Bureaucracies, and Public Sector Careers." In *Gender, Bureaucracy, and Democracy*, edited by Mary M. Hale and Rita Mae Kelly. Westport, CT: Greenwood Press.

———, 1989b. "Women in Management and Public Sector Careers." In *Gender, Bureaucracy, and Democracy*, edited by Mary M. Hale and Rita Mae Kelly. Westport, CT: Greenwood Press.

Hale, Mary M., Rita Mae Kelly, and Jayne Burgess, 1989. "Women in Arizona Executive Branch of Government." In *Gender, Bureaucracy, and Democracy*, edited by Mary M. Hale and Rita Mae Kelly. Westport, CT: Greenwood Press.

Hall, Grace, and Alan Saltzstein, 1977. "Equal Employment Opportunity for Minorities in Municipal Government." *Social Science Quarterly*, vol. 57 (March), pp. 864–872.

Hargrove, Erwin C., and John C. Glidewell, 1990. *Impossible Jobs in Public Management*. Lawrence: University Press of Kansas.

Hawkins, Keith, and Peter K. Manning, forthcoming. *Legal Decision-Making*.

Hellriegel, Don, and Larry Short, 1972. "Equal Employment Opportunity in the Federal Government: A Comparative Analysis." *Public Administration Review*, vol. 32 (November/December), pp. 851–867.

Henderson, Lenneal J., 1979. *Administrative Advocacy: Black Administrators in Urban Bureaucracy*. Palo Alto, CA: R&E Research Associates.

———, 1988. "Urban Administrators: The Politics of Role Elasticity." In *Urban Minority Administrators: Politics, Policy, and Style*, edited by Albert K. Karnig and Paula D. McClain. Westport, CT: Greenwood Press.

Herbert, Adam W., 1974. "The Minority Administrator: Problems, Prospects, and Challenges." *Public Administration Review*, vol. 34 (November/December), pp. 556–563.

Hill, Larry, 1976. *The Model Ombudsman*. Princeton, NJ: Princeton University Press.

————, 1992. *The State of Public Bureaucracy.* Armonk, NY: M.E. Sharpe.

Hindera, John J., 1990. *Representative Bureaucracy: Are Active and Passive Representation Linked?* Unpublished Ph.D dissertation, University of Houston.

————, 1993a. "Representative Bureaucracy: Imprimis Evidence of Active Representation in the EEOC District Offices." *Social Science Quarterly*, vol. 74, (March), pp. 95–108.

————, 1993b. "Representative Bureaucracy: Further Evidence of Active Representation in the EEOC District Offices." *Journal of Public Administration Research and Theory*, vol. 3 (October), pp. 415–429.

Holmes, Steven A. 1995. "Programs Based on Sex and Race Are under Attack: Dole Seeks Elimination." *The New York Times*, 16 March, p. 1A.

Holzler, Jim, FmHA Oklahoma Rural Housing Loans Program, 1995. Telephone interview by author, 21 February. Athens, GA.

Hornblower, Margot, 1995. "Taking It All Back: At Pete Wilson's Urging, the University of California Says No to Racial Preferences." *Time*, vol. 146 (July 31), pp. 34–35.

Housing Act of 1949. United States Code, 1964. Vol. 42, secs. 502–504.

Hraba, Joseph, 1994. *American Ethnicity.* 2nd edition. Itasca, IL: F.E. Peacock.

Hula, Richard C., 1991. "Neighborhood Development and Local Credit Markets." *Urban Affairs Quarterly*, vol. 27 (December), pp. 249–267.

Hurh, Won Moo, and Kwang Chung Kim, 1989. "The 'Success' Image of Asian Americans: Its Validity, and Its Practical and Theoretical Implications." *Ethnic and Racial Studies*, vol. 12 (October), pp. 512–538.

Ingraham, Patricia W., and Carolyn R. Ban, 1986. "Models of Public Management: Are They Useful to Federal Managers in the 1980s?" *Public Administration Review*, vol. 46 (March/April), pp. 152–160.

Ingraham, Patricia W., and David H. Rosenbloom, 1990. "Political Foundations of the American Federal Service: Rebuilding a Crumbling Base." *Public Administration Review*, vol. 50 (March/April), pp. 210–219.

Jackson, Mary R., and Robert W. Jackson, 1986. "Racial Inequalities in Home Ownership." In *Race, Ethnicity, and Minority Housing in the United States*, edited by Jamshid A. Momeni. Westport, CT: Greenwood Press.

Jacobs, Barry G., Kenneth R. Harney, Charles L. Edson, and Bruce S. Lane, 1986. *Guide to Federal Housing Programs.* 2nd edition. Washington, D.C.: The Bureau of National Affairs.

Johnson, Cathy Marie, and Georgia Duerst-Lahti, 1992. "Public Work, Private Lives." In *Women and Men of the States: Public Administrators at the State Level*, edited by Mary E. Guy. Armonk, NY: M.E. Sharpe.

Jones, Hezekiah S., 1994. "Federal Agricultural Policies: Do Black Farm Operators Benefit?" *The Review of Black Political Economy*, vol. 22 (Spring), pp. 25–50.

Kahn, Robert L., Donald M. Wolfe, Robert P. Quinn, and J. Diedrick Snoek, 1964. *Organizational Stress: Studies in Role Conflict and Ambiguity.* New York: John Wiley & Sons.

Karnig, Albert K., and Paula D. McClain, 1988. "Minority Administrators: Lessons from Practice." In *Urban Minority Administrators: Politics, Policy, and Style*, edited by Albert K. Karnig and Paula D. McClain. Westport, CT: Greenwood Press.

Katzmann, Robert A., 1980. *Regulatory Bureaucracy: The Federal Trade Commission and Antitrust Policy*. Cambridge, MA: MIT Press.

Kaufman, Herbert, 1956. "Emerging Conflicts in the Doctrines of Public Administration." *The American Political Science Review*, vol. 50 (December), pp. 1057–1073.

Kawar, Amal, 1989. "Women in Utah Executive Branch of Government." In *Gender, Bureaucracy, and Democracy*, edited by Mary M. Hale and Rita Mae Kelly. Westport, CT: Greenwood Press.

Kellough, J. Edward, 1989. *Federal Equal Employment Opportunity Policy and Numerical Goals and Timetables: An Impact Assessment*. New York: Praeger.

———, 1990a. "Integration in the Public Workplace: Determinants of Minority and Female Employment in Federal Agencies." *Public Administration Review*, vol. 50 (September/October), pp. 557–566.

———, 1990b. "Federal Agencies and Affirmative Action for Blacks and Women." *Social Science Quarterly*, vol. 71 (March), pp. 83–92.

Kellough, J. Edward, and Euel Elliott, 1992. "Demographic and Organizational Influences on Racial/Ethnic and Gender Integration in Federal Agencies." *Social Science Quarterly*, vol. 73 (March), pp. 1–11.

Kellough, J. Edward, and David H. Rosenbloom, 1992. "Representative Bureaucracy and the EEOC: Did Civil Service Reform Make a Difference?" In *The Promise and Paradox of Civil Service Reform*, edited by Patricia W. Ingraham and David H. Rosenbloom. Pittsburgh, PA: University of Pittsburgh Press.

Kim, Pan Suk, 1993. "Racial Integration in the American Federal Government: With Special Reference to Asian-Americans." *Review of Public Personnel Administration*, vol. 8 (Winter), pp. 52–66.

Kim, Pan Suk, and Berhanu Mengistu, 1994. "Women and Minorities in the Work Force of Law-Enforcement Agencies." *American Review of Public Administration*, vol. 24 (June), pp. 161–179.

Kingdon, John W., 1984. *Agendas, Alternatives, and Public Policies*. Glenview, IL: Scott, Foresman.

Kingsley, J. Donald, 1944. *Representative Bureaucracy*. Yellow Springs, OH: Antioch Press.

Kivisto, Peter, 1995. *Americans All: Race and Ethnic Relations in Historical, Structural, and Comparative Perspectives*. Belmont, CA: Wadsworth.

Koutsoyiannis, A., 1977. *Theory of Econometrics*. 2nd edition. New York: Barnes and Noble.

Kranz, Harry, 1976. *The Participatory Bureaucracy: Women and Minorities in a More Representative Public Service*. Lexington, MA: Lexington Books.

Krause, George A., 1996. "The Institutional Dynamics of Policy Administration Bureaucratic Influence over Securities Regulation." *American Journal of Political Science*, vol. 40 (November), pp. 1083–1121.

Krislov, Samuel, 1974. *Representative Bureaucracy*. Englewood Cliffs, NJ: Prentice-Hall.

Krislov, Samuel, and David H. Rosenbloom, 1981. *Representative Bureaucracy and the American Political System*. New York: Praeger.

Larson, Arthur, 1973. "Representative Bureaucracy and Administrative Responsibility: A Reassessment." *Midwest Review of Public Administration*, vol. 7 (April), pp. 79–89.

Levine, Charles H., B. Guy Peters, and Frank J. Thompson, 1990. *Public Administration: Challenges, Choices, Consequences.* Glenview, IL: Scott, Foresman/Little, Brown Higher Education.

Levitan, David M., 1946. "The Responsibility of Administrative Officials in a Democratic Society." *Political Science Quarterly*, vol. 61 (December), pp. 562–598.

Lewis, Eugene, 1980. *Public Entrepreneurship: Toward a Theory of Bureaucratic Political Power.* Bloomington: Indiana University Press.

Lewis, Gregory B., 1988. "Progress Toward Racial and Sexual Equity in the Federal Civil Service?" *Public Administration Review*, vol. 48 (May/June), pp. 700–706.

———, 1990. "In Search of Machiavellian Milquetoast: Comparing Attitudes of Bureaucrats and Ordinary People." *Public Administration Review*, vol. 50 (March/April), pp. 220–227.

Lewis, Gregory B., and David Nice, 1994. "Race, Sex, and Occupational Segregation in State and Local Governments." *American Review of Public Administration*, vol. 24 (December), pp. 393–410.

Lewis, William G., 1989. "Toward Representative Bureaucracy: Blacks in City Police Organization, 1975–1985." *Public Administration Review*, vol. 49 (May/June), pp. 257–268.

Lipset, Seymour Martin, 1992. "Equal Chances Versus Equal Rights." *Annals of the American Academy of Political and Social Science*, vol. 523, pp. 63–74.

Lipsky, Michael, 1972. "Street-Level Bureaucracy and the Analysis of Urban Reform." In *Blacks and Bureaucracy: Readings in the Problems and Politics of Change*, edited by Virginia B. Ermer and John H. Strange. New York: Thomas Y. Crowell Company.

———, 1980. *Street-Level Bureaucracy: Dilemmas of the Individual in Public Services.* New York: Russell Sage Foundation.

Long, Norton, 1949. "Power and Administration." Reprinted in *Public Administration: Concepts and Cases*, edited by Richard J. Stillman. Boston: Houghton Mifflin.

———, 1952. "Bureaucracy and Constitutionalism." *American Political Science Review*, vol. 46 (September), pp. 808–818.

Lowi, Theodore, 1969. *The End of Liberalism.* New York: Norton.

Lukes, Steven, ed., 1986. *Power.* Washington Square, NY: New York University Press.

McClain, Paula D., 1993. "The Changing Dynamics of Urban Politics: Black and Hispanic Municipal Employment—Is There Competition?" *Journal of Politics*, vol. 55, 2 (May), pp. 399–414.

McClain, Paula D., and Albert K. Karnig, 1988. "Introduction: Minority Administrators—Another Frontier." In *Urban Minority Administrators: Politics, Policy, and Style*, edited by Albert K. Karnig and Paula D. McClain. Westport, CT: Greenwood Press.

———, 1990. "Black and Hispanic Socioeconomic and Political Competition." *American Political Science Review*, vol. 84, no. 2 (June), pp. 535–545.

McCubbins, Mathew, Roger G. Noll, and Barry Weingast, 1987. "Administrative Procedures as Instruments of Political Control." *Journal of Law, Economics, and Organization*, vol. 3, pp. 243–277.

———, 1989. "Structure and Process as Solutions to the Politicians' Principal-Agency Problem." *Virginia Law Review*, vol. 74, pp. 431–482.

Marini, Frank, ed., 1971. *Toward a New Public Administration: The Minnowbrook Perspective*. Scranton, PA: Chandler.

Martin, Thad, 1985. "The Disappearing Black Farmer." *Ebony*, vol. 40 (June), pp. 145–150.

Martinez, Thomas R., 1991. "The Role of Hispanic Public Administration: A Theoretical and Empirical Analysis." *American Review of Public Administration*, vol. 21 (March), pp. 33–56.

Massey, Douglas S., 1979. "Effects of Socioeconomic Factors on Residential Segregation of Blacks and Spanish Americans in U.S. Urbanized Areas." *American Sociological Review*, vol. 44 (December), pp. 1015–1022.

Mazmanian, Daniel A., and Paul A. Sabatier, 1989. *Implementation and Public Policy*. Lanham, MD: University Press of America.

Meier, Kenneth J., 1975. "Representative Bureaucracy: An Empirical Analysis." *American Political Science Review*, vol. 69 (June), pp. 526–542.

———, 1980. "Measuring Organizational Power: Resources and Autonomy of Government Agencies." *Administration and Society*, vol. 12 (November), pp. 357–375.

———, 1991. *The Politics of Hispanic Education*. Albany: State University of New York Press.

———, 1993a. "Latinos and Representative Bureaucracy: Testing the Thompson and Henderson Hypotheses." *Journal of Public Administration Research and Theory*, vol. 3 (October), pp. 393–414.

———, 1993b. *Politics and the Bureaucracy: Policymaking in the Fourth Branch of Government*. 3rd edition. Pacific Grove, CA: Brooks Cole.

———, 1993c. "Representative Bureaucracy: A Theoretical and Empirical Exposition." *Research in Public Administration*, vol. 2, pp. 1–35.

Meier, Kenneth J., and Lloyd Nigro, 1976. "Representative Bureaucracy and Policy References: A Study in the Attitudes of Federal Executives." *Public Administration Review*, vol. 36 (July/August), pp. 458–469.

Meier, Kenneth J., and Kevin B. Smith, 1994. "Representative Democracy and Representative Bureaucracy: Examining the Top-Down and Bottom-Up Linkages." *Social Science Quarterly*, vol. 75 (December), pp. 790–803.

Meier, Kenneth J., and Joseph Stewart, Jr., 1992. "The Impact of Representative Bureaucracies: Educational Systems and Public Policies." *American Review of Public Administration*, vol. 22 (September), pp. 157–171.

Meier, Kenneth J., and Joseph Stewart, Jr., and Robert England, 1989. *Race, Class, and Education*. Madison: University of Wisconsin.

Miller, George A., and L. Wesley Wager, 1971. "Adult Socialization, Organizational Structure, and Role Orientations." *Administrative Science Quarterly*, vol. 16 (June), pp. 151–163.

Mladenka, Kenneth R., 1989a. "Barriers to Hispanic Employment Success in 1,200 Cities." *Social Science Quarterly*, vol. 70 (June), pp. 391–407.

———, 1989b. "Blacks and Hispanics in Urban Politics." *American Political Science Review*, vol. 83 (March), pp. 165–191.

———, 1991. "Public Employee Unions, Reformism, and Black Employment in 1,200 American Cities." *Urban Affairs Quarterly*, vol. 26 (June), pp. 532–548.

Moe, Terry, 1987. "An Assessment of the Positive Theory of 'Congressional Dominance.'" *Legislative Studies Quarterly*, vol. 12 (November), pp. 475–520.

Momeni, Jamshid A., 1986. "The Housing Conditions of Black Female-Headed Households: A Comparative Analysis." In *Race, Ethnicity, and Minority Housing in the United States*, edited by Jamshid A. Momeni. Westport, CT: Greenwood Press.

Mosher, Frederick, 1982. *Democracy and the Public Service*. 2nd edition. New York: Oxford University Press.

———, 1992. "Public Administration Old and New: A Letter from Frederick C. Mosher." *Journal of Public Administration Research and Theory*, vol. 2 (April), pp. 199–202.

Murray, Sylvester, Larry D. Terry, Charles A. Washington, and Lawrence F. Keller, 1994. "The Role Demands of Minority Public Administrators: The Herbert Thesis Revisited." *Public Administration Review*, vol. 54 (September/October), pp. 409–417.

Myrdal, Gunnar, 1969. *An American Dilemma*. New York: Harper and Row.

Nachmias, David, and David H. Rosenbloom, 1973. "Measuring Bureaucratic Representation and Integration." *Public Administration Review*, vol. 33 (November/December), pp. 590–597.

———, 1980. *Bureaucratic Government USA*. New York: St. Martin's Press.

Nalbandian, John, 1989. "The U.S. Supreme Court's 'Consensus' on Affirmative Action." *Public Administration Review*, vol. 49, pp. 38–45.

Nathan, Richard P., and Charles Adams, 1976. "Understanding Central Hardship." *Political Science Quarterly*, vol. 91 (Spring), pp. 47–62.

———, 1989. "Four Perspectives on Urban Hardship." *Political Science Quarterly*, vol. 104 (Fall), pp. 483–508.

Nelson, Aaron G., Warren F. Lee, and William G. Murray, 1973. *Agricultural Finance*. 6th edition. Ames: The Iowa State University Press.

Niskanen, William A., 1971. *Bureaucracy and Representative Bureaucracy*. Chicago: Aldine.

O'Hare, William P., 1990. "A New Look at Asian Americans." *American Demographics*, vol. 12, pp. 26–31.

O'Hare, William P., and Judy C. Felt, 1991. *Asian Americans: America's Fastest Growing Minority Group*. Washington, D.C.: Population Reference Bureau.

Okun, Arthur M., 1975. *Equality and Efficiency: The Big Tradeoff*. Washington, D.C.: The Brookings Institution.

Ostrom, Vincent, 1973. *The Intellectual Crisis in American Public Administration*. Tuscaloosa: University of Alabama Press.

O'Sullivan, Elizabethann, and Gary R. Rassel, 1995. *Research Methods for Public Administrators*. 2nd edition. White Plains, NY: Longman Publishers.

Page, Paul, 1994. "African-Americans in Executive Branch Agencies." *Review of Public Personnel Administration*, vol. 14 (Winter), pp. 25–50.

Pennington, Debra, FmHA Georgia Rural Housing Loans Program, 1994. Personal interview by author, 21 June. Athens, GA.

Perry, James L., 1996. "Measuring Public Service Motivation: An Assessment of Construct Reliability and Validity." *Journal of Public Administration Research and Theory*, vol. 6, pp. 5–22.

Perry, James L., and Lois R. Wise, 1990. "The Motivational Bases of Public Service." *Public Administration Review*, vol. 50, pp. 367–373.

Pindyck, Robert S., and Daniel L. Rubinfeld, 1991. *Econometric Models and Economic Forecasts*. 3rd edition. New York: McGraw-Hill.

Pitkin, Hanna F., 1967. *The Concept of Representation*. Berkeley: University of California Press.

Prottas, Jeffrey M., 1979. *People Processing: The Street-Level Bureaucrat in Public Service Bureaucracies*. Lexington, MA.: Heath.

Rainey, Hal G., 1982. "Reward Preferences Among Public and Private Managers: In Search of the Service Ethic." *American Review of Public Administration*, vol. 50, (Winter), pp. 288–302.

————, 1991. *Understanding and Managing Public Organizations*. San Francisco: Jossey-Bass.

Redford, Emmette S., 1969. *Democracy in the Administrative State*. New York: Oxford University Press.

Reno, Lee P., 1970. *Pieces and Scraps: Farm Labor Housing in the United States*. Washington, D.C.: Rural Housing Alliance.

Riccucci, Norma M., 1986. "Female and Minority Employment in City Government: The Role of Unions." *Policy Studies Journal*, vol. 15 (September), pp. 3–15.

Ripley, Randall B., and Grace A. Franklin, 1991. *Congress, the Bureaucracy, and Public Policy*. 5th edition. Pacific Grove, CA: Brooks Cole.

Ringquist, Evan J., 1995. "Political Control and Policy Impact in EPA's Office of Water Quality." *American Journal of Political Science*, vol. 39 (May), pp. 336–363.

Rohe, William M., and Michael A. Stegman, 1994. "The Impact of Home Ownership on the Social and Political Involvement of Low-Income People." *Urban Affairs Quarterly*, vol. 30 (September), pp. 152–172.

Rohr, John A., 1986. *To Run a Constitution: The Legitimacy of the Administrative State*. Lawrence: University Press of Kansas.

Romzek, Barbara S., and J. Stephen Hendricks, 1982. "Organizational Involvement and Representative Bureaucracy: Can We Have It Both Ways." *American Political Science Review*, vol. 76, pp. 75–82.

Rose, Winfield H., and Tiang Ping Chia, 1978. "The Impact of the Equal Employment Opportunity Act of 1972 on Black Employment in the Federal Service: A Preliminary Analysis." *Public Administration Review*, vol. 38 (May/June), pp. 245–251.

Rosenblatt, Robert A., Dwight Morris, and James Bates, 1992. "Blacks Lead in Rejections for Home Loans." *Los Angeles Times*, 6 September, p. 1(A).

Rosenbloom, David H., 1973. "A Note on Interminority Group Competition for Federal Positions." *Public Personnel Management*, vol. 2 (January/February), pp. 43–48.

————, 1993. *Public Administration: Understanding Management, Politics, and Law in the Public Sector*. 3rd edition. New York: McGraw-Hill.

Rosenbloom, David H., and Jeannette G. Featherstonhaugh, 1977. "Passive and Active Representation in the Federal Service: A Comparison of Blacks and Whites." *Social Science Quarterly*, vol. 57 (March), pp. 873–882.

Rosenbloom, David H., and Douglas Kinnard, 1977. "Bureaucratic Representation and Bureaucratic Behavior: An Exploratory Analysis." *Midwest Review of Public Administration*, vol. 11 (March), pp. 35–42.

Rourke, Francis E., 1978. *Bureaucratic Power in National Politics*. 3rd edition. Boston: Little, Brown.

———, 1992. *Bureaucracy, Politics, and Public Policy*. 3rd edition. Boston: Little, Brown.

Saltzstein, Grace Hall, 1979. "Representative Bureaucracy and Bureaucratic Responsibility: Problems and Prospects." *Administration and Society*, vol. 10 (February), pp. 464–475.

———, 1983. "Personnel Directors and Female Employment Representation." *Social Science Quarterly*, vol. 64, pp. 734–746.

———, 1985. "Conceptualizing Bureaucratic Responsiveness." *Administration and Society*, vol. 17 (November), pp. 283–306.

———, 1986. "Female Mayors and Women in Municipal Jobs." *American Journal of Political Science*, vol. 30 (February), pp. 140–164.

———, 1992. "Bureaucratic Responsiveness: Conceptual Issues and Current Research." *Journal of Public Administration Research and Theory*, vol. 2 (January), pp. 63–88.

Schick, Allen, 1975. "The Trauma of Politics: Public Administration in the Sixties." In *Past, Present, and Future*, edited by Dwight Waldo. University: The University of Alabama Press.

Schneider, Anne, and Helen Ingram, 1993. "Social Construction of Target Populations: Implications for Politics and Policy." *American Political Science Review*, vol. 87, pp. 334–348.

Scholz, John T., Jim Twombly, and Barbara Headrick, 1991. "Street-Level Political Controls over Federal Bureaucracy." *American Political Science Review*, vol. 85 (September), pp. 829–850.

Schroeder, Richard, 1993. "Progress Is Slow on Minority Loans; Rejection Rate for Blacks Still High Despite Area Lenders' Special Efforts." *The Buffalo News*, 28 November, p. 12 (Business).

Scott, Patrick G., 1997. "Assessing Determinants of Bureaucratic Discretion: An Experiment in Street-Level Decision Making." *Journal of Public Administration Research and Theory*, vol. 7 (January), pp. 35–57.

Shafritz, Jay M., Albert C. Hyde, and David H. Rosenbloom, 1986. *Personnel Management in Government: Politics and Process*. 3rd edition. New York: Marcel Dekker.

Shalala, Donna E., and J.A. McGeorge, 1981. "The Women and Mortgage Credit Project: A Government Response to the Housing Problems of Women." In *Building For Women*, edited by Suzanne Keller. Lexington, MA: Lexington Books.

Sherwood, Frank, 1990. "The Half-Century's 'Great Books' in Public Administration." *Public Administration Review*, vol. 50 (March/April), pp. 249–264.

Shumavon, Douglas H., and H. Kenneth Hibbeln, 1986. "Administrative Discretion: Problems and Prospects." In *Administrative Discretion and Public Policy Implementation*, edited by Douglas H. Shumavon and H. Kenneth Hibbeln. New York: Praeger.

Sigelman, Lee, and Albert K. Karnig, 1976. "Black Representation in the American States: A Comparison of Bureaucracies and Legislatures." *American Politics Quarterly*, vol. 4 (April), pp. 237–246.

Silk, Mark, 1993. "Fighting to Hold on to His Farmland." *Atlanta Constitution*, 2 March, Section A, p. 3.

Simon, Herbert, 1947. *Administrative Behavior: A Study of Decision-Making Processes in Administrative Organizations*. New York: Macmillian.

Smith, Russell, 1980. "Representative Bureaucracy: A Research Note on Demographic Representation in State Bureaucracies." *Review of Public Personnel Administration*, vol. 1 (Fall), pp. 1–14.

Snipe, C. Matthew, and Alan L. Sorkin, 1986. "American Indian Housing: An Overview of Conditions and Public Policy." In *Race, Ethnicity, and Minority Housing in the United States*, edited by Jamshid A. Momeni. Westport, CT: Greenwood Press.

Squires, Gregory, ed., 1992. *From Redlining to Reinvestment*. Philadelphia: Temple University Press.

——, 1994. *Capital and Communities in Black and White: The Intersections of Race, Class, and Uneven Development*. Albany: State University of New York Press.

Squires, Gregory D., and Sunwoong Kim, 1995. "Does Anybody Who Works Here Look Like Me: Mortgage Lending, Race, and Lender Employment." *Social Science Quarterly*, vol. 76 (December), pp. 823–838.

Stanley, Jeanie R., 1989. "Women in Texas Executive Branch of Government." In *Gender, Bureaucracy, and Democracy*, edited by Mary M. Hale and Rita Mae Kelly. Westport, CT: Greenwood Press.

Stegman, Michael, 1985. "New Financing Programs for Housing." In *The Unsheltered Woman: Women and Housing in the 80's*, edited by Eugenie Birch. New Brunswick, NJ: The State University of New Jersey.

Stein, Lana, 1985. "A Representative Protection Service: Concept, Demand, Reality." *Review of Public Personnel Administration*, vol. 5 (Summer), pp. 78–89.

——, 1986. "Representative Local Government: Minorities in the Municipal Work Force." *The Journal of Politics*, vol. 48 (August), pp. 694–713.

——, 1994. "Privatization, Work-Force Cutbacks, and African-American Municipal Employment." *American Review of Public Administration*, vol. 24 (June), pp. 181–191.

Stillman, Richard J., 1992. "The Rise of U.S. Bureaucracy." In *Public Administration: Concepts and Cases*, edited by Richard J. Stillman. Boston: Houghton Mifflin.

Subramanian, V., 1967. "Representative Bureaucracy: A Reassessment." *American Political Science Review*, vol. 61 (December), pp. 1010–1019.

Sue, Derald Wing, 1989. "Racial/Cultural Identity Development among Asian-Americans: Counseling/Therapy Implications." *AAPA Journal*, vol. 13, pp. 80–86.

——, 1994. "Asian-American Mental Health and Help-Seeking Behavior." *Journal of Counseling Psychology*, vol. 41, pp. 292–295.

Tamerius, Karin L., 1995. "Sex, Gender, and Leadership in the Representation of Women." In *Gender Power, Leadership, and Governance*, edited by Georgia Duerst-Lahti and Rita Mae Kelly. Ann Arbor: University of Michigan Press.

Taylor, Frederick, 1911. *Principles of Management*. New York: Norton.

Thielemann, Gregory S., and Joseph Stewart, Jr., 1996. "A Demand-Side Perspective on the Importance of Representative Bureaucracy: AIDS, Ethnicity,

Gender, and Sexual-Orientation." *Public Administration Review*, vol. 56 (March/April), pp. 168–173.

Thompson, Frank J., 1976. "Minority Groups in Public Bureaucracies: Are Passive and Active Representation Linked?" *Administration and Society*, vol. 8 (August), pp. 201–226.

————, 1978. "Civil Servants and the Deprived: Socio-Political and Occupational Explanations of Attitudes Toward Minority Hiring." *American Journal of Political Science*, vol. 22 (May), pp. 325–347.

Turner, Ralph B., 1956. "Role-Taking, Role Standpoint, and Reference-Group Behavior." *The American Journal of Sociology*, vol. 61 (January), pp. 316–328.

United States Commission on Civil Rights, 1965. *Equal Opportunity in Farm Programs*. Washington, D.C.: GPO.

————, 1979. *The Federal Fair Housing Enforcement Effort*. Washington, D.C.: GPO.

————, 1980. *Success of Asian Americans: Fact or Fiction?* Washington, D.C.: GPO.

————, 1982. *The Decline of Black Farming in America*. Washington, D.C.: GPO.

United States Department of Agriculture, Farmers Home Administration, 1979. Subsidy Repayment Agreement (FmHA 1951–I Exhibit A). Washington, D.C.: GPO.

————, 1982. *Credit Reference Information* (FmHA-GA 1910–1). Washington, D.C.: GPO.

————, 1984. *A Brief History of the Farmers Home Administration*. Washington, D.C.: GPO.

————, 1985. *Rural Housing Application Interview* (FmHA Instruction 1944–A Exhibit D). Washington, D.C.: GPO.

————, 1987. *Statement Required by the Privacy Act* (FmHA 410–9). Washington, D.C.: GPO.

————, 1990. *This Is FmHA* (Program Aid 973). Washington, D.C.: GPO.

————, 1991. *Budget and/or Financial Statement* (FmHA 1944–3). Washington, D.C.: GPO.

————, 1992. *Application for Rural Housing Assistance (Non-Farm Tract)* (FmHA 410–4). Washington, D.C.: GPO.

————, 1993a. *Application Assistance Guide for Rural Housing Loan Request*. Washington, D.C.: GPO.

————, 1993b. *Credit History Work Sheet*. Washington, D.C.: GPO.

————, 1993c. *Guaranteed Rural Housing Loans* (Program Aid 1501). Washington, D.C.: GPO.

————, 1993d. *Request for Verification of Employment* (FmHA 1910–5). Washington, D.C.: GPO.

United States Department of Commerce, Bureau of the Census, 1994. *Statistical Abstract of the United States 1994*. 114th edition. Washington, D.C.: GPO.

United States General Accounting Office, 1979. *Farmers Home Administration and Small Business Administration Natural Disaster Loan Programs: Budget Implications and Beneficiaries* (August 6, 1979). Washington, D.C.: GAO.

———, 1993. *Rural Housing: FmHA's Home Loan Program Not Meeting the Needs of All Rural Residents* (RCED-93–57). Washington, D.C.: GAO.

United States Government Manual 1993/1994, 1993. Washington, D.C.: Office of the Federal Register, National Archives and Records Administration.

Van Riper, Paul, 1958. *History of the United States Civil Service.* New York: Harper and Row.

Waldo, Dwight, 1952. "Development of a Theory of Democratic Administration." *American Political Science Review*, vol. 46 (March), pp. 81–103.

———, 1971. "Some Thoughts on Alternatives, Dilemmas, and Paradoxes in a Time of Turbulence." In *Public Administration in a Time of Turbulence*, edited by Dwight Waldo. Scranton, PA: Chandler.

———, 1980. *The Enterprise of Public Administration: A Summary View.* Novato, CA: Chandler & Sharp.

Wamsley, Gary L., Robert N. Bacher, Charles T. Goodsell, Philip S. Kronenberg, John A. Rohr, Camilla M. Stivers, Orion F. White, and James F. Wolf, 1990. *Refounding Public Administration.* Newbury Park, CA: Sage.

Warner, Rebecca L., Brent S. Steel, and Nicholas P. Lovrich, 1989. "Conditions Associated with the Advent of Representative Bureaucracy." *Social Science Quarterly*, vol. 70, pp. 562–578.

Weingast, Barry R., 1984. "The Congressional Bureaucratic System: A Principal-Agent Perspective." *Public Choice*, vol. 32, no. 3, pp. 147–191.

Weingast, Barry R., and Mark J. Moran, 1983. "Bureaucratic Discretion or Congressional Control? Regulatory Policymaking by the Federal Trade Commission." *Journal of Political Economy*, vol. 91, pp. 765–800.

———, 1984. "The Myth of the Runaway Bureaucracy: The Case of the FTC." *Regulation*, vol. 6, pp. 22–28.

Weiss, R.S, 1980. "Housing for Single Parents." In *Housing Policies for the 1980s*, edited by Roger Montgomery and Dale Rogers Marshall. Lexington, MA: Lexington Books.

Welch, Susan, Albert K. Karnig, and Richard A. Eribes, 1983. "Changes in Hispanic Local Public Employment in the Southwest." *The Western Political Science Quarterly*, vol. 36 (December), pp. 660–673.

Widmer, Candace, 1993. "Role Conflict, Role Ambiguity, and Role Overloads on Boards of Directors of Nonprofit Human Service Organizations." *Nonprofit and Voluntary Sector Quarterly*, vol. 22 (Winter), pp. 339–356.

Wildavsky, Aaron, 1988. *The New Politics of the Budgetary Process.* Glenview, IL: Scott Foresman.

Willoughby, William F., 1919. *The Government of Modern States.* New York: D. Appleton-Century.

———, 1927. *Principles of Public Administration, with Special Reference to National and State Governments of the United States.* Baltimore, MD: Johns Hopkins.

Wilson, Woodrow, 1887. "The Study of Administration." Reprinted in *Public Administration: Concepts and Cases*, edited by Richard J. Stillman. Boston: Houghton Mifflin.

Wise, Lois R., 1990. "Social Equity in Civil Service Systems." *Public Adminis-tration Review*, vol. 50 (September/October), pp. 567–575.

Wyatt, Nancy, and Gerald M. Phillips, 1988. *A Case Study of the Farmers Home Administration: Studying Organizational Communication*. Norwood, NJ: Ablex.

Wynia, Bob L., 1974. "Federal Bureaucrats' Attitudes Toward Democratic Ideol-ogy." *Public Administration Review*, vol. 34 (March/April), pp. 156–162.

Index

About the Author

Sally Coleman Selden received her doctorate in public administration at the University of Georgia and in 1996 won the American Political Science Association's Leonard D. White award for the best doctoral dissertation in the field of public administration. This book is based on that doctoral project. At the Maxwell School of Citizenship and Public Affairs, Syracuse University, Professor Selden teaches courses in public management, human resource management, and organizational theory.